Focus on Teachers' Centres

Focus on Teachers' Centres

Christopher Redknap

NFER Publishing Company Ltd.

Published by the NFER Publishing Company Ltd.,
Darville House, 92–93 Peascod Street,
Windsor, Berks. SL4 1DF
Registered Office: The Mere, Upton Park, Slough, Berks.
SL1 2DQ
First published 1977
© C. Redknap 1977
ISBN 0 85633 126 0

Typeset by Preface Ltd.,
Salisbury, Wilts.
Printed in Great Britain by
The Whitefriars Press Ltd., London and Tonbridge.
Distributed in the USA by Humanities Press Inc.,
Atlantic Highlands, New Jersey 07716 USA.

Contents

ACKNOWLEDGEMENTS

My thanks are due to Professor Vernon Mallinson, who was my tutor when I wrote the original version of this text for my MEd thesis at Reading University. I also owe a debt of gratitude to Mr G. Geoghegan and his staff at the Education Library of Reading University School of Education, who for many years have patiently responded to my requests for help.

Teachers' Centres rely for their success on cooperation, and I am extremely grateful to all those who have given me their co-operation in the formulation of this study. These include teachers' centre leaders and other educationalists in the four countries considered, and I am particularly grateful to the colleagues from overseas who wrote me such lengthy reports of their work. I have also appreciated the hospitality shown by the staff of teachers' centres that I visited in my search for information. I owe a special debt of gratitude to the wardens of the teachers' centres in Berkshire, and to all those who have contributed to the growth of the Centre at Maidenhead for their unflagging professional support and personal encouragement.

Finally my thanks are due to my Mother and other relatives for their patience, to Jane Taylor, Kathleen Leigh-Pierce, Ann Hay and other friends who helped me in my work, and to Rosa Bayliffe who has so painstakingly undertaken the typing connected with this study.

PREFACE

It is hoped that this study which has been kept as uncomplicated as possible will be of relevance to those who have a general interest in education at home and abroad. In addition I hope that those who have been intimately involved in teachers' centre work will find that it acts as a reminder of grassroots' developments already accomplished and of problems waiting to be solved.

Following my general introduction to the 'centre' concept, the first five chapters of this study are concerned with the history, prevailing influences, context, and functions of teachers' centres in England and Wales, followed by a description of the links between the centres and other educational agencies. There then ensues a consideration of the role of teachers' centres in the light of the James Report (DES, 1972) and the developments that have followed its publication.

Although the 'focus' of this study is biased in favour of the teachers' centres in England and Wales, the contents of Chapters 7, 8 and 9 show that this phenomenon is not unique to this island. Teachers' centres in three widely differing countries — the USA, Norway and Kenya are described so as to give readers a comparative dimension and reference points for more detailed consideration of the centres in this country.

Throughout the book, extracts from speeches and writings of many educationalists have been included in order to illustrate the wealth and variety of the contributions that have been made to the teachers' centre movement.

I hope that the detailed list of references and the bibliography that follows will enable interested readers to pursue further their study of teachers' centres which in some areas seem already imperilled even before they have hardly been given time to prove their worth.

INTRODUCTION

Before this contemporary and international subject is considered, it may be helpful to reflect on some of the less specific connotations surrounding the meaning of the word 'centre'. A focal point is brought to mind, or maybe we draw parallels with the heart. It may imply the drawing together of material or imaginary lines, or we may contemplate a core or kernel. On the other hand a gathering around a nucleus may suggest itself, and a middle position would seem to be important. As a further suggestion perhaps the meaning lies in the point of concentration. In all these less specific considerations, a centre seems to be concerned with amalgamation and meeting.

This general exploration may help to clarify our thoughts on centres, but it also draws our attention to the present popularity of the word as a title. We may think of leisure centres, entertainment centres, social centres, recreation centres, or sports centres; alternatively it may be a youth centre, health centre, or garden centre that springs to mind. It seems that despite the variety of centres, in all the establishments a prime aim is to encourage a coming together of people to share activity, company, experiences and expertise.

When we turn from centres of a diverse nature to the more specific ones that are the subject of this study, we are still confronted with variety even in nomenclature. By merely searching through some of the relevant literature, in addition to the norm 'teachers' centre' we find other titles, such as 'curriculum development centre', 'county centre', 'resource and technology centre', 'education centre', 'education development centre', 'teachers' resources centre', 'advisory centre', 'pedagogic centre', 'research and development centre', 'curriculum studies centre', 'experimental centre', 'development centre', 'in-service training centre', and 'schools development centre'. This varied list contains some clues to the nature and function of teachers' centres, and also suggests that within the term 'teachers' centre' may lie a hidden concept that at one and the same time is both simple and complex.

Having focussed attention on the meaning surrounding the word 'centre', extended our thoughts to examples of other centres, and drawn attention to the fact that 'teachers' centre' is not a title that is exclusively used, it may be helpful to list some definitions and analogies that have been used in connection with the subject of this study —

'A place to pool ideas' (Sandilands, 1971)

'an institution that is geared to respond to, and to satisfy the professional needs of teachers in the area in which it is located.' (Culling, 1974)

'local physical facilities, and self-improvement programs organized and run by teachers themselves for the purpose of upgrading educational performance'. (Bailey, 1971)

'an incubator for ideas, an informal centre, a work-shop — and at least a social centre'. (Curry, 1968)

'the hub of a wheel of activities'. (Schools Council, Pamphlet No 6, 1970)

These descriptions may provoke thought and interest, but they also suggest that we need to be clear about what we mean by a 'teachers' centre'. Professor Geoffrey Matthews has said that:

'A good working definition (of a Teachers' Centre) is a meeting-place for at least two people concerned with learning'. (Matthews in Thornbury (Ed), 1973)

However, on that basis a teachers' centre is a school staff room, a media resources centre, or an education library. But a youth centre does not exist in a coffee bar, on the street corner, or on a soccer pitch, and neither do the first illustrations satisfy enough criteria to be called teachers' centres. In order to qualify for the title some deliberate and conscious attempt must have been made to provide accommodation, which has as its main function the provision of professional improvement facilities for serving teachers. The sponsoring bodies may vary, and other professionals may be given help, but teachers' centres give top priority to teachers at the 'coal-face'.

Chapter 1

The Development of Teachers' Centres in England and Wales

Even though the number of teachers' centres in this country has grown at an amazing rate from the early Sixties to the present when there are approximately 550 centres, their existence cannot be accepted without an examination of some of the events that led up to, and accompanied their 'birth and childhood'. The reasons for holding meetings have changed, but through the centuries, teachers like most groups of professionals, have felt the need to improve their competence. For example:

'Some two hundred and fifty years ago, outstanding charity school-masters like Henry Dixon were formulating courses to raise their own standard of efficiency' (Edmonds, 1958).

These early attempts failed, because of a rather different historical development — the Jacobite cause — but setbacks that were to confront later teachers would be more easily overcome.

In the nineteenth century one of the stimuli that encouraged teachers to involve themselves in in-service education, although of a casual nature, was the desire to meet the requirements of the Inspectorate. For some the motivation may have been self-protective, but for many there was a desire to support parent-voluntary societies who undertook to organize courses that would improve learning and teaching standards.

One of the influences on in-service provision in Victorian times was the system of payment by results. This led to the organization by local school boards of courses on subjects that earned the greater rewards. Despite this biased provision there were specific developments. In 1848 the College of Preceptors was awarded a royal charter so that it could further in-service training and in 1888 the Educational Development Association was founded. This latter body established a policy and the machinery for teacher initiated and led in-service education.

The nineteenth century also produced Pupil-Teachers' Centres, which in some ways foreshadowed the arrival of teachers' centres in the twentieth century. It was after the demise of the monitorial system pioneered by Bell and Lancaster that a space was left in teaching provision, but the illness of a Norfolk schoolmaster in 1838 gave Sir James Kay-Shuttleworth the idea that was to lead to the growing involvement of pupil-teachers in education. When the schoolmaster was unable to teach he was very adequately replaced by a boy of fourteen. Sir James was so impressed by this success that he allowed the boy to continue teaching even after the schoolmaster's recovery, and similar appointments were made by other workhouses. Soon after this a visit made to Holland by Sir James confirmed his faith in a pupil-teacher system. He saw how the Dutch schools of the Society for the Public Good had adopted a scheme that was an adaptation of the monitorial system. In return for a teaching commitment, promising Dutch youngsters were able to continue their studies for an extra two or three years.

When the first English pupil-teachers were engaged, their teaching hours were unlimited, but regulations were gradually introduced to make it possible for them to study more, and to receive more instruction. Although headteachers were responsible for the pupil-teachers' education, many were neither sufficiently scholarly or dedicated to carry out their obligations. In the words of one pupil-teacher:

'Many Head-teachers were unequal to very advanced coaching, and many others had but little energy for anything beyond the ordinary calls of the school. . . . Quite seventy-five per cent of the pupil-teachers received less tuition than they were entitled to'. (Christian, 1922)

It was generally realized that exceptionally gifted teachers were needed to guide the pupil-teachers, and in the 1870s the movement towards the establishment of Pupil-Teachers' Centres was gathering support. The first Centre appeared in 1881, and three years later measures were introduced that required pupil-teachers to teach only half-time, and enabled them to receive instruction during the day, instead of only in the evenings and on Saturdays. Typical premises for these centres were converted private homes, and among the subjects for females was 'the art of teaching'. In 1884 the Royal Commissioners reported that:

> 'Central reference libraries have been provided for pupil teachers, and a small sum per head per annum is devoted by the Board to their extension. . . .'

— and even in those early days, it was recognized that travel subsidy was needed —

> 'Omnibus tickets are given from a private source to those pupil-teachers who come from a distance but only on condition of their regular attendance at the classes'. (*ibid.*)

Attendance at Pupil-Teacher Centres provided specialist help from more qualified teachers, and it also gave the young people opportunities to share experiences with their contemporaries, and in so doing prevent avoidable isolation. However, with the expansion of both teachers' training colleges and secondary education the pupil-teacher system became less relevant. Pupil-Teacher Centres were gradually phased out, especially after the 1902 Education Act, which extended secondary education, and set the starting age for pupil-teachers in urban areas at sixteen years of age, and at fifteen in rural areas. Nevertheless some Centres remained, and a Government Committee set up in 1923 recommended that:

> 'Pupil-Teacher Centres in urban areas should be abolished, though a system of rural pupil-teachership might for the present be allowed to continue.' (Birchenough, 1938)

Continue they did, for it was not until 1939 that the last Pupil-Teacher Centre at Watford was closed.

As the pupil-teacher organization declined, qualified teachers began to show a greater desire for self-improvement. Union backing for in-service training has played a significant part in the growth of teachers' professional self-renewal, for from the NUT's refresher courses, and in-service gatherings were learnt many of the lessons that have influenced more recent innovations,

Only five years after the closing of the last Pupil-Teachers' Centre at Watford, and as the Second World War was drawing to a close, the McNair Report (Board of Education, 1944) was published, which put forward proposals for the establishment of a building to which serving teachers could turn for support and advice:

> 'The main building of the school, separated possibly from other university buildings, should be so equipped with libraries, conference rooms and other amenities that it becomes the Centre of the professional interests of practising teachers in the area, and the place to which LEAs and other bodies concerned with education would look for accommodation and guidance in the matter of public lectures, conferences, discussion groups, exhibitions, and other means of promoting the interests of education'.

In 1948 McNair's proposed Institutes and Area Training Organizations were set up, but these 'centres of professional interest for practising teachers' seemed reluctant to appear. Some teachers did begin to make more use of Institute facilities, and links between ATO organizers and the schools grew up informally as a result of two-way participation, but only the London Institute established an Education Centre by its constitution, and later described it in London University's Calendar 1971 as:

> 'An Education Centre, which should serve as a Centre of interest and activity for practising teachers, members and officers of LEAs and others concerned with education, more especially within the area'.

It would seem that this constitution has been fully acted upon for as Ethel M. Thompson reported in 1972:

> 'The Teachers' Centre at the London Institute is, and has

been, a meaningful place of educational activities for practising teachers. It is not merely a library or conference room, but a source of immediate practical advice and help. It satisfies, it would seem, the McNair recommendations and the needs of the teachers'.

The Centre's current programme (University of London, 1977) includes details of informal activities, short courses, conferences, vacation courses, and award-bearing courses. The staff includes an Adviser to Teachers, one Deputy Adviser for Secondary Education, one Deputy Adviser for Primary Education, and an Administrative Assistant. In 1976 the Centre moved into more spacious and better equipped accommodation, and so its impact should soon become even greater.

The University Centre for Teachers at the London Institute, seems to have followed the pattern suggested by McNair, but in 1952 a rather different centre was established, but this too was to be a 'landmark' in the evolution of teachers' centres. This, the Martineau Centre was set up by Birmingham Education Committee, in part to compensate its teachers for not being provided with a special allowance, such as had recently been granted to teachers in London. Whereas the London Institute's Centre came into being as a response to an academic need and the recommendations of a government report, the Martineau Centre grew out of social and economic needs, caused by urbanization to make up for possible cultural and environmental shortcomings, and to provide an alternative to the 'lonely bed-sitter'. The Martineau Centre was established at a cost of thirty-eight thousand pounds. A 1955 article in *Education* (Martineau Teachers Club, 1955) described the scene:

'apart from the courses at the Centre, there are social amenities which include an attractive tearoom, a large lounge with an inner bar leading to a glass-covered terrace and extensive gardens, a smoke room, a sitting room, a library, and reading room. . . There is a music-room . . . an audiovisual aids room . . . a craft room . . . a drama room . . . A Resident Warden, paid by the LEA coordinates the activities'.

Local needs demanded that social facilities should be an attraction, but despite this bias, a model of LEA support with an entrepreneurial warden in charge of a base for professional support was to be a strong influence on the teachers' centres 'not yet born'.

While cities like Birmingham were recovering from the ravages of World War II, and the subsequent shortages of manpower and resources, a greater interest in possible changes in the curriculum of the schools was emerging. As with many other initiatives taken in the preceding century, the USA was leading the way. In 1946 a conference was held in Chicago, and the deliberations that took place then, and following the related report in 1950, stirred many educationalists to begin a review of established practice and curriculum.

Among groups most concerned with this review were specialist professional associations such as the Mathematical Association, and the associations connected with the teaching of science. In 1955 the Mathematical Association's report 'The Teaching of Mathematics in Primary Schools' was published, and it promoted unprecedented interest among teachers from all types of school. This report is mentioned because a consideration of this period could be dominated completely by Russia's launching of Sputnik, that one could ignore the fact that even before this startlingly successful technological achievement, a reappraisal of some areas of the curriculum had begun.

However, despite developments prior to 1957 there is no doubt that:

'The dramatic success of Sputnik is associated in many minds with the recognition of the need to bring about a rapid improvement of the educational system in order to support technological advance and economic growth'. (Schools Council, 1973)

The launching of Sputnik is an example of a technological advance that was to influence educational change, but this historic event was accompanied by the publication of studies which showed that the teachers themselves could have an impact on the innovative process. In 1961 the Science Masters Association and the Association of Women Science Teachers (later to become the Association for Science Education), drew up proposals for a new GCE Science course and examination. On this occasion, technological and educational needs were not to be ignored because of economic constraints — the Nuffield Foundation offered funds to finance the work, so courses for other teachers were planned and the new materials began to emerge.

The Mathematical Association, the Association for Science Education, together with other groups of teachers such as those responsible for the School Mathematics Project are examples of progressive groups that have accelerated change. However, their deliberations took place at a time of radical change, following Sputnik, and at a time which, as Joslyn Owen said at the Fourth National Conference for Teachers' Centre Leaders, coincided with 'The golden age of education's literature about change in the USA.' (Wardens in the South West and Exeter University, 1974)

At this time the most important project related to the English teachers' centre movement evolved from the interest caused by 'The Teaching of Mathematics in Primary Schools' report. (The Mathematical Association, 1955). The Nuffield Foundation's investment in secondary school science had met with a favourable response, so the Ministry of Education was asked if a similar project on the teaching of mathematics to younger children could be launched. The Ministry agreed, and in August 1963 the Assistant Director of the Nuffield Foundation asked Professor Geoffrey Matthews if he would be interested in researching more relevant materials for children between the ages of eight and thirteen years (this was quickly altered to five to thirteen years). He accepted the invitation and began to devise a strategy for the project.

The British Association sent out a circular asking for help in the search for a base from which Professor Matthews could work, and the offer of rooms in the top floor of the New City School, Newham, was soon forthcoming. When Professor Matthews claims that this 'fast became the first operational teachers' centre' (Matthews in Thornbury (ed), 1973), it must be assumed that he means the first of the type to be set up for workshop work connected with a particular project.

When chief education officers were invited to propose pilot areas for the project there were over one hundred replies, so a second letter was circulated. This time, stricter conditions were laid down, and these included the stipulation that each pilot area should have a centre with someone in charge to coordinate the development work. Although some of the original volunteers withdrew at this stage, the project team were still able to be highly selective, as only fourteen areas were to be involved at the initial stages. The original centres in these pilot areas were sited in varied accommodation but the basic requirement was that there should be a work area, a discussion room, and a refreshment area. From the beginning:

> 'The vital point was that the Centre should be seen to be run by and for the teachers; one of the most successful Centres seemed to have every teacher for miles around on the Committee.' (*ibid.*)

— so a pattern of involvement and participation was fixed.

So many of the LEAs were disappointed because they had been excluded that seventy-seven 'Second Phase Areas' were admitted to the Project. These areas also set up centres as did forty-four 'Continuation Areas' which joined later. From the beginning, teachers' groups took an active part in the project's work, as they evaluated activities and themes suggested for the Teachers' Guides. Teachers were vocal in their praise and their criticism, as they experimented with the materials themselves, and also worked with children in infant, junior and secondary schools.

The Nuffield Mathematics Project provides an important chapter in the story of teachers' centres. Its contribution influenced considerably the setting up of future centres, but the Project's impact has further implications. The growth of teachers' centres, like that of many other British establishments, has been on the whole haphazard, but in the case of those connected with the early stages of Professor Matthews' Project, an element of forced obligation was exerted on the original volunteer local authorities. The obligation hastened action, and made these few years numerically and ideologically important in the growth of a teachers' centre network across the country. In addition, the response between local and national levels of responsibility in education was an example of cooperation that is significant when one considers the advantages and disadvantages of a decentralized educational system.

In *Centre* the former Newsletter of the National Conference of Teachers' Centre Leaders (Cartwright, 1975), John Litson refers to the Nuffield Maths and Science Projects as the 'supposed joint sires to the centres', and so the second 'sire' needs some introduction. As with the Mathematics Project, the scene had been set for innovation by the publication of several reports, that indicated that our curriculum in this area was in need of reappraisal. Examples of these publications are the Ministry of Education Pamphlet Number 42, 'Science in the Primary School' (1961), and the Educational Supply Association's publication 'Approaches to Science in the Primary School' (1960). Also, other curriculum development projects had been set up by the Ministry of Education and the British Association, but the Nuffield Junior Science Project directed by Mr Ron Wastnedge, was to have the greatest impact on the growth of teachers' centres. Launched in 1964 with twelve local authority pilot areas, teachers worked from centres set up on similar lines to the Nuffield Mathematics Centres. The trials took place in 1965 and 1966, and in 1966 thirty-five additional local authorities became involved in the work. Now, thirteen years after the project was started, activities initiated by its leaders are still being developed by individual teachers, and by further project teams. However, it has been claimed that as far as this project was concerned:

'The teachers' centres were probably the most important development of all. The exchange of ideas was stimulating and the range of activities which could go on there went beyond the boundaries of science, or mathematics, or even beyond the range of the primary school itself, for in the teachers' centres, primary and secondary teachers could meet and help each other'. (Schools Council Curriculum Bulletin, 1970)

Just as in the early Sixties educationalists were concerned with the science and mathematics provision in our schools, so also was there a great interest in our examination system. In 1960 the Beloe Committee had forwarded proposals for secondary school examinations, other than GCE, and in 1961, the Certificate of Secondary Education Standing Committee was formed. As a result, plans for CSE were considered, and from the start there was a regional, local and school orientation to these examinations. Teachers had the opportunity to mould these examinations to suit the needs of their pupils, and those who took advantage of this opportunity often became more deeply involved in the curricular needs of the schools. CSE thus gave a boost to the professional competence of secondary school teachers, and also made them consider problems on a local basis, so that where multi-purpose teachers' centres were set up, these colleagues were more prepared for involvement in curriculum development.

The Secondary Schools Examination Council (SSEC) had existed since 1917, but its progress had been somewhat restricted because examinations were separated from the curriculum. In 1962, at a time when curricular change was a topic of general concern, the Minister of Education, then Sir David Eccles, set up within his Ministry a 'Curriculum Study Group' of HMIs, specialists from Institutes of Education, LEA Inspectors, teachers, and administrators. The purpose of the group was to offer advice and information to the schools, and technical services to the SSEC. The CSG immediately attracted fury from the teachers' associations and other quarters, on the grounds that the Ministry appeared to be taking a central control over the curriculum, which had in England and Wales been traditionally free from government interference.

Because of this criticism, the new Minister, Sir Edward Boyle, chaired a meeting at which the need for new cooperative machinery to deal with school curricula and examinations was discussed. The outcome of this meeting was that a Working Party, under the chairmanship of Sir John Lockwood, was asked to make a report. In March 1964, the Working Party made its proposals, which were accepted by the teachers' associations and the LEAs, and so yet another Minister, Mr Quintin Hogg, now Lord Hailsham, was invited to implement its recommendations. This he did, and in October 1964 the Schools Council for Curriculum and Examinations was set up. A basic feature of the body was that the membership of the Governing Council and its major committees, was to contain a majority of teachers, who became members through their professional associations.

The 'birth' of the Schools Council is described in detail, because of the early and often lasting links that have existed between the Council and the teachers' centres of this country. The Council has been described as a 'national teachers' centre,' and local teachers' centres generally act as agencies for Schools Council work. In many ways the partnership symbolizes the balance between national and local interest in education, but it especially underlines the importance of teacher participation in curricular affairs. However, teacher autonomy has been dramatically brought to the notice of the public at large by events at, among other places, William Tyndale Junior School and this curriculum control is one of the many topics under discussion in the current national debate on education. (DES, 1976)

A matter of urgent concern for the newly formed Schools Council was the preparation needed in readiness for the raising of the school leaving age to sixteen. Plans were made in the hope that some of the previous mistakes and omissions could be avoided. In the Council's second Working Paper, suggestions were made for this impending reorganization, and among these suggestions was one which read —

'Centres should be set up, based on schools, where teachers could think through the problems of ROSLA, arriving at solutions which they could apply with real conviction'. (Schools Council Working Paper 2, 1965)

In addition, the Paper gave news of support for centres that went beyond words:

'The Council appreciates the difficulties at a time of teacher shortage, but education authorities might like to know that the DES has already agreed that any authority that is establishing a Pilot Scheme need not count against the quota any teachers released for this purpose.' (*ibid.*)

The way seemed clear for the introduction of centres, which could offer more help and support to colleagues in secondary schools.

So far as teachers' centres were concerned, an even more important Schools Council Working Paper was to appear in 1967. Entitled 'Curriculum Development: Teachers' Groups and Centres', it gave practical suggestions for the establishment and organization of teachers' centres, and it was made perfectly clear in this pamphlet, which happened to be 'a little red book', that the Schools Council was enthusiastically in favour of these establishments:

'The Council's hope is that teachers will more and more, meet in groups to discuss curriculum problems, and that LEAs will do all that is practicable to encourage such groups, and in particular, help them with the use of such accommodation, apparatus, and secretarial assistance as may be necessary'. (Schools Council, 1967)

It was reported that the LEAs were taking action to implement the recommendations within a few days of the pamphlet's publication.

In 1960 the number of teachers' centres was small; in 1967 there were two hundred and seventy, and between 1967 and 1972, over three hundred more centres were set up. This sharp increase cannot be wholly attributable to Working Paper 10, but the figures do suggest that its advice was heeded, and that this advice was written and read at a time when an accumulation of events, moods, and trends were combining to hasten innovative action regarding teachers' centres.

Chapter 2

National Character Influences on the Development of Teachers' Centres in England and Wales

It might be expected that establishments that have a relatively short history, and which have by and large sprung up at a phenomenal rate within a single decade would conform to a fairly predictable pattern. A tour of any group of teachers' centres would soon destroy any vision of uniformity (see the Appendix). The centres vary in size, leadership, organization, staffing, resources and programme, and they have been set up in premises that range from temporary classrooms to civil defence buildings, from old town halls to attics, and from lecture rooms to disused huts. As with most other features of the British educational scene, diversity would seem to hold the key, but when we consider the geographical and historical factors influencing the development of our system, this characteristic should cause no surprise:

'Insular security, of course, has been the chief factor in shaping and determining the characteristic philosophy and outlook of the British people. The insular situation has made political unity a possibility, a rich diversity of flourishing and unfettered sub-group cultures that stimulate the whole nation a reality, a spirit of compromise over burning controversial questions inescapable, a rich common tradition that includes wide ranges of common experience (and that therefore is distrustful of intellectualism and of 'professional' interference) the mainspring of all action'. (Mallinson, 1975)

Just as this security has enabled school systems to be organized differently in different areas, it has also enabled teachers' centres to respond to these school systems, and to local circumstances, in ways that are often varied and sometimes idiosyncratic. Our daily changing climate, our increasingly varied ethnic origins, and our terrain which changes so quickly within a small area, may all be influences on the teachers' centre network as a whole, and on the differences between each individual centre. Such differences may present administrative problems and perplex visitors from more uniformly organized educational systems, but for those who hold great hopes for the future of teachers' centres, it is on these differences that much of their potential depends. 'The promise of the Centres is that they will reflect what can succeed in *this* town, and this village'. (Thompson, 1972)

In the book *In-Service Education and Teachers' Centres* (edited by Elizabeth Adams, 1975), John Brand describes the role of teachers' centres and supports the claim that the influence of geographical factors has had a great influence on the wide range of differences between one teachers' centre and another. Teachers' centres (to prepare for the Schools Council analogy) are 'very young plants', but according to a conference report:

'Centres took root and grew where attention was given to the local circumstances. To ignore these circumstances, to seek to impose a model based upon theory unrelated to what local people saw as their needs, carried the danger of inhibiting a natural process of development'. (Schools Council Pamphlet, 1970)

It is perhaps a fortunate that no 'model based upon theory' has been foisted on local centres, for in England and Wales this move would run counter to a strong philosophical influence on the educational system. Empiricism has held sway, and unlike countries that have a shorter educational history, the character of education has been influenced largely by experience rather than theory.

The question of centralization has already been mentioned when the formation of the Schools Council was being described, but in this more general consideration of teachers' centres in a national context it also deserves attention. In a centralized system it is necessary to organize for change that can be implemented regardless of local circumstances. This fact not only makes for very generalized legislation, but also inhibits risk-taking, for any mistakes made are bound to cause widespread dislocation. Furthermore, a country that has a tradition of centralized decision-making will probably have schools that are staffed by teachers, who are only capable of receiving instructions and acting upon them. On the other hand, in a decentralized system, teachers should have been prepared to participate in changes that do not ignore local circumstances, the individual needs of children, and the strengths and weaknesses of particular schools. An additional implication of the centralization versus decentralization issue, so far as teachers' centres are concerned, is that in a centralized system the transmission of official policy through mass lectures may be appropriate, whereas in a decentralized system the search for local solutions to problems may more easily be found in practical workshop sessions.

This emphasis on the importance of the individual teacher in a potentially innovative situation reminds us that the story of the British educational system is full of individuals who have impressed their own personalities on their schools, and on their pupils. Those with the responsibility for the leadership of schools have generally had more opportunities for innovation, but it is in the traditional autonomy of the British headteacher that many of the strengths and weaknesses of the schools lie. This autonomy has affected the degree of encouragement that colleagues have received for teachers' centre involvement, but it has also influenced the evolution of the teachers' centre warden's role. As head of an educational establishment he has acquired or assumed much of the autonomy ascribed to a headteacher, and in a system that has laid great store on the development of leadership qualities he has been able to impress his own personality on the progress of the centre. It will be interesting to see whether the teachers' centre impetus can be maintained when the generation of wardens who used this autonomy to 'put teachers' centres on the educational map' are for one reason or another no longer in initiative-taking positions.

Britain has traditionally allowed freedom to individuals and groups, especially of minority interests, but it is also the home of parliamentary democracy. Though lacking the 'trappings' of parliament, the democratic ideal is reflected in teachers' centres for as Brian Oastler said at the Fourth National Conference for Teachers' Centre Leaders held at Exeter in 1974, they are

'almost exclusively and uniquely in theory, democratically organized institutions. They are run by teachers for teachers with a steering committee, management body, or council which consists of a majority of teacher representatives'. (Wardens in the South West, 1974)

The organization of democracy varies from centre to centre, and such variation is an example of a characteristic of teachers' centres already described, but on the whole teachers have ample opportunities to participate in the organization of their centre. When decisions are being taken, the democratic process and the position of an autonomous leader, could result in conflict, but on the whole, our characteristic love of compromise and common sense prevails to produce acceptable solutions.

Teacher involvement in curriculum development, and participation in teachers' centre activities had demanded a greater degree of professionalism than has sometimes been required in the past, and this has been to the good. However, this increased professionalism in some ways runs counter to a character trait often identifiable in British educators:

'we tend to be amateurs who muddle through, rather than planners with a clearly defined and undeviating purpose in view: . . . We are at our best when improvising, and to improvise we draw on a lengthy tradition of self-discipline and voluntary cooperation'. (Mallinson, 1975)

Despite this apparent conflict, there is much to be seen in the development of teachers' centres that supports this claim for amateur status, and *adhocian* organization. The leaders are often selected for their classroom 'know-how' rather than their academic background; their programmes often contain practical sessions at which improvisation and ingenuity are encouraged;

and above all most of their accommodation is now functional as a result of much imaginative adaptation and improvization.

Intuition has guided much of this improvization, and in an age of statistics, theory, and questionnaires it is heartening to discover that less measurable qualities have also been at work. Teachers' centres will no doubt need to become more involved in educational research and management, and theories of learning and teaching will increasingly influence their work but against a background of early 'learning by mistakes' and 'following our noses' it is to be hoped that the importance of good personal relationships, and the more subjective aspects of education will not be forgotten.

An ability to improvize may have been caused by the independence engendered by our islandic position, but this insularity may also have given rise to an approach to education that is by and large conservative. Change has come about by gradual adjustment rather than by revolution, and this adjustment is also a reflection of the way in which our governmental structure changes. However, the needs of society have been changing with such increasing rapidity, that it is possible that the establishment of teachers' centres, although almost 'telescoped' into a single decade, will provide the means by which further changes can be achieved through a combination of *laissez-faire* evolution, and more imposed innovation. As this happens, the decision-makers will do well to be reminded of these words from an Australian —

'a social institution is a product of unique, and historical influences' (Bassett, 1970)

for much of the current discussion concerning education has been triggered off by an apparent national inability to organize its affairs successfully.

Chapter 3

Changes in Educational Thinking that have Accompanied and Influenced the Development of Teachers' Centres in England and Wales

Just as a review of the historical development of teachers' centres in England and Wales needs to be accompanied by a description of some of the relevant national characteristics influencing their nature, so also should it be linked with a consideration of some of the educational principles influencing the schools they serve. The centres are sometimes physically linked to schools, and sometimes in separate accommodation, but in either case their programmes should always reflect, and sometimes initiate changes in education's psychological, sociological, and philosophical thinking. If teachers' centres are to survive they cannot be left in a learning and teaching vacuum.

After the Great Education Act of 1870, the main aim of education was to get children to school, and then teach them a rudimentary body of knowledge that would equip them for a job in a world that was rapidly becoming industrialized. Since then human aspirations have been greatly extended, and technological advance has increased at a greater pace than had previously been thought possible:

> 'We live in an exciting age — an age in which human knowledge is growing at an ever-accelerating pace. It has been estimated that in 1830 human knowledge doubled every fifty years, whilst by the 1960s it is doubling every ten years. By 1970 it will be doubling every five years. We certainly know how difficult it is to keep abreast of new knowledge, new techniques, and new ideas'. (Curry, 1968)

In such an age it is no longer possible to be confident about what knowledge should be transmitted through education, although an increasing number of attempts are now being made to find some agreement that will aid progression. Many teachers have aimed to teach children how to learn rather than what to learn, so that they are able to continue learning as the frontiers of knowledge are further extended. Teachers' centres have arranged activities that allow teachers to work as children might work in investigatory situations so that they can acquire study skills and research techniques, together with a joy in learning that will have an impact on them and on their pupils. The centres have also extended their facilities, so that teachers can have access to a wide range of resource materials.

Just as there has been a general 'explosion' of knowledge, so has there been an increase in the more specific knowledge of how children learn. The work of child psychologists has 'shed light' on child development, and so more effort has been made to cater for the individual needs of children. As each child has been given more attention, a more child-centred approach to education, influenced by the work of Froebel, Rousseau, Montessori, Dewey, Susan Isaacs and others, has emerged:

> 'through the whole period of concentration on child-centredness, and down to the present Piaget dominated era of the Sixties, primary teachers have been given regular opportunities to acquaint themselves with psychological developments'. (Johnston, 1971)

This acquaintance has not only come through course attendance, but also through visits to schools, exhibitions of children's work, and through making investigations in 'teacher-centred' ways.

Schools that have adopted a 'child-centred' approach have been led on to more informal ways of working, and this informality is reflected in many teachers' centres, where there is importance given to good personal relationships, and where many of the sessions give opportunities for personal involvement. Just as in an 'informal' classroom one might find some children weighing, others reading, some making a model, and so on, so in an informal teachers' centre you might find, for instance, some teachers painting, others photocopying, and some playing the recorder, and so on. In informal classrooms, children find it hard to differentiate between work and play, and in many teachers' centres, there is also this lack of differentiation.

Piaget and other influential leaders of educational thought placed great stress on the importance of learning from direct experience, and the ways in which children learn through the use of materials. Teachers' centre courses have helped teachers develop these ideas, but they have also provided them with direct experiences — for example examining a wood-louse under a microscope — and with work with materials — for example making a crude horse from two logs and some dowelling. It is hoped that these experiences will give teachers new insights, and increase sensitivity rather than merely provide them with new skills and techniques.

As the curriculum has been re-examined in the light of fresh knowledge of how children learn, more efforts have been made to add 'relevance' to the child's day. This addition has meant that the case for dividing knowledge into subject areas has become less valid. In a book about the Schools Council, Richard Pring lists some of the criticisms of a timetable that is based on subject divisions:

'What has been called the 'compartmentalization of knowledge' by the Plowden Report, 'the artificial separation' of parts by R.O.S.L.A. Number One, 'the atomization of knowledge' by Wheeler in 'Curriculum Process', was referred to in Schools Council documents as 'an imprisonment by the disciplines', 'a fragmented type of curriculum', 'an artificial restriction', 'the pigeon-holing of knowledge', 'subject prejudice'. (Pring in Bell and Prescott (eds), 1975)

In multi-purpose teachers' centres where there are no heads of departments, or subject examinations pressures, colleagues have often found 'common ground' that has enabled them to meet challenges with a less 'blinkered' view.

At visits made to teachers' centres some teachers have been encouraged to consider more cooperative approaches to teaching. Teachers' centres depend on the cooperation of their clientele, and this cooperation is similar to that which is needed for the success of team teaching approaches. At a Schools Council Regional Studies Conference held at Clacton in 1972 Mr. I. J. McCulloch highlighted this cooperation:

> 'Already Teachers' Centres represent a considerable development in the support to teachers' work in schools, especially in the concept of cooperation not just in buildings, and resources (important though these are).'

The cooperation involved in teachers' centre work, and team teaching organization both lead to increased participation — in schools between pupils and teacher — and in centres between professional and professional.

A form of cooperation which has been advocated by Reports that are linked with the names of Newsom (DES, 1963), Gittens (DES, 1967a), and Plowden (DES, 1967b), is that which should exist between home and school. This emphasis has accompanied the rise of educational sociology, the publication of surveys like those carried out by Stephen Wiseman for the Plowden Committee, and Young and McGeeny (1968), and the demand from some parents that they should be given a greater share in the education of their children. This parental demand has been accentuated to some extent by the influence of the mass media, which has brought schooling more attention through an increased television, radio and newspaper coverage of educational matters. As the general public has become better informed about education, some teachers may have become less secure, and so involvement in teachers' centres' activities has served both to increase their knowledge, and to add to their expertise. In addition, some centres have attracted support and interest from those who are not teachers. By this willingness to interest a wider 'market', teachers' centres may help to break down further barriers between home and school, and between social worker and teacher, while at the same time decreasing the isolation of teachers which was criticized strongly by McNair in 1944.

A further important trend in education since 1945 has been the reduction of mechanisms which differentiate between, and label children. Many secondary modern and grammar schools have been succeeded by comprehensive schools; middle schools have introduced new age group organization into state schools; and many 'A', 'B', and 'C' Forms have been re-organized into mixed-ability groups. In some schools horizontal has given way to vertical grouping. Re-organization has forced many teachers to re-consider their methods and beliefs, and they have often had to show great flexibility in this re-consideration process. With their short history teachers' centres have not had time to acquire a rigid structure, and so they have often been fitting meeting places for re-consideration gatherings.

Organizational frameworks can be fairly easily identified, but changes in attitude are not exposed so easily. As society as a whole, and the educational institutions within it, have struggled towards greater egalitarianism, there have been accompanying changes within the teaching profession:

'What is important to notice is the changes which already are taking place in the teachers — changes we can't do much to alter either, because the new young teachers entering the staff-room, enter them already changed — they grew into adolescence to the sound of the young Beatles, not like many of us to the sound of doodlebugs, and air-raid sirens, and when it comes to conflict between staff and students they have tendency to be, as the Head would put it, on the wrong side. For the day of the Dominie is past — we are entering a period which might be called the Meister dammerung, the twilight of the masters. The dominant genes of the bandmaster teacher have been replaced by the recessive genes of the quiet guitar strummer — and whatever the older teacher may say, we can't change our personalities'.

This 'colourful' extract from a speech made by Professor H. A. Ree at the Fourth National Conference of Teachers' Centre Leaders (Wardens of the South-West, 1974) places the attitudes and appearance of teachers in a societal context, and draws attention to the changing nature of authority since World War Two. It may well be that teachers' centres, which through accident and/or design emerged as non-hierarchical institutions, will have an influential part to play in the reassembling of authority patterns.

In the Sixties and early Seventies many teachers' centre activities were planned to introduce teachers to additions to the curriculum with which they were unfamiliar. However, as the Warden of Hackney Teachers' Centre has illustrated (Richards, F., 1975) it has become increasingly necessary for these additions to be arranged in some sort of framework so that duplication is avoided and structure and sequence emphasized. The re-emergence of structure as a priority concern has come at a time of extreme financial stringency which has also seen a re-emphasis of the so-called 'basic subjects'. At many centres teachers are meeting together to thrash out 'core' curriculum issues, and in doing so clear up some of the misunderstandings that accompanied the turmoil of expansionist years.

Chapter 4

Teachers' Centres in England and Wales

a) As bases for in-service education and training

Although we have become used to calling colleges where students are prepared for a teaching career, colleges of education or higher education rather than teachers' training colleges, the term 'in-service' training has been retained, but 'in-service education' is now more widely used. This co-existence exemplifies the philosophical arguments entwined within the 'education and training' debate, but in this consideration of the role of teachers' centres, no choice between the two terms need be made, for most centres offer both in-service education and training, and differences between the two are often indistinguishable. For example some teachers want and need to be trained to use an electronic stencil cutter, or to operate a sixteen millimetre projector, and many centres arrange training sessions that are suitable for this purpose. At these sessions, a teacher may begin by merely watching and copying a model, but then as he begins to understand how the equipment works, and how it can be used in a school setting, he becomes involved in the process of education. In addition, teachers' centres offer colleagues opportunities to extend their education in areas such as environmental studies, modern mathematics, and the language arts, through lectures, discussion groups and workshop sessions.

Most centre leaders work out their priorities for in-service courses in consultation with their users, and with the cooperation of their sponsors. In this regard, it is interesting to note how the marrying of education and training can benefit both the employer and the employee. In-service training would seem to produce a more skilled employee who is a classroom practitioner, whilst in-service education should contribute towards the development of a professional who is capable of initiating further learning experiences for himself and for others.

Many teachers received their preparation for teaching over twenty years ago, so when we consider the changes that have taken place in all branches of learning, even in the past few years, it will soon become evident that a continuous injection of in-service education and training is necessary, if our schools are to keep pace with the worldwide 'explosion of knowledge and aspirations'. In addition many other teachers undertook initial training at a time of teacher shortage when colleges were restricted in their selection of entrants, and it may be that a concerted effort will have to be made through in-service education to raise the professional and academic standards of more teachers.

Not only have prospective and practising teachers attempted to keep pace with the general extension of the knowledge barriers, they have also tried to master an increasing number of professional skills that enable them to keep abreast of educational advances. The NFER Report *The Objectives of Teacher Education* (Leeds University, Institute of Education) published in 1973, includes a list of one hundred and twenty-nine professional skills that are needed by teachers of children in their middle years of schooling. The list includes objectives such as 'fostering language growth particularly in linguistically deprived children', and 'knowledge of procedure for requisitioning books'. The existence of such a battery of skills underlines the need for professional education that is not terminated at the end of the initial training period, especially as the list will alter as new developments occur.

From their inception most teachers' centres have accepted as their responsibility the task of providing some in-service training opportunities, especially as many of them grew out of Nuffield Maths or Science Centres where curriculum development and in-service training were intermeshed. Once teachers' centres had been set up, it was less often necessary to organize courses in classrooms where —

'amid the smell of cabbage, dead milk bottles and decaying

raincoats we would have tea and a Marie biscuit before settling down to a study of someone's second-hand hobby-horse'. (Pollard, 1970)

However some teacher centre initiated in-service training is still based in schools so that any suggested changes can be related to a particular school's circumstances.

When one studies the course descriptions in teachers' centre bulletins and circulars it is evident that the programmes have been influenced by the early Nuffield emphasis on the practical and relevant, and the demands from teachers who beg for help with day to day problems. From random selections of courses advertised by six widely scattered teachers' centres, we find sessions entitled 'Basic Skills in Music-making', 'Overhead Projector Workshop', 'Pottery for Beginners', 'The Importance of Language in the Development and Education of Young Children', 'The Creative Use of Paper', and 'Worship in the Secondary School'. Such courses aim both at adding new skills to the teachers' repertoire, and at increasing awareness of educational developments.

As the coordinator and organizer of the teachers' centre programme, many leaders try to plan this programme with the requests of their users in mind. There has been a concerted effort to provide what the teachers want, but as Desmond F. Hogan pointed out at the 1974 Exeter Conference for Teachers' Centre Leaders:

'the headache sufferer may 'want' a pain reliever but may 'need' a pair of spectacles, just as a secondary teacher may 'want' the latest information on problems of work with radio isotopes, but may 'need' a radical re-training in teaching method.'

This possible dilemma seems to demand that programme planning should be a cooperative task, and that teachers' centre leaders need a strong theoretical and practical training for the 'facilitating function'.

The Brian Cane (1969) study of teachers' views and preferences for in-service training reveals that the priority topics for most teachers were those that came under the headings 'teaching methods', 'aids and materials', and 'the development of new teaching schemes and programmes'. Similarly, Harriet Townsend's DES survey of in-service training for teachers, carried out in 1967 with seven thousand teachers and published in 1970, showed that when asked what they would like to do when they used the teachers' centre, seven per cent said they wanted to take part in miscellaneous activities, 75 per cent said they wanted to practise with new materials and techniques, 65 per cent said they wanted to help with the development of local curriculum materials, 72 per cent said they wanted to try out new materials, and 77 per cent said they wanted to exchange ideas and experiences with their colleagues. These research studies both showed that the majority of teachers are most interested in activities that give help that can be acted upon immediately.

A consideration of the more specific demands from teachers reveals that the most frequently requested subject areas are again those that have a practical bias. When the former Warden of Enfield Teachers' Centre sent out a questionnaire asking for suggestions for courses, art and craft, mathematics, science and reading were the subjects for which there were most requests, and the Warden adds a postscript to the findings — 'The appetite of teachers for Art and Craft especially seems to be insatiable'. (Khan in Thornbury (ed), 1973) In support of these general returns, June Braithwaite reports that:

> 'The Workshop sessions most in demand are often on Mathematics, Primary Science, Art and Craft, and the teaching of reading'. (Braithwaite, 1971)

An investigation carried out in the West Midlands by G. Lawrence in 1974 again showed that reading was the area in which most teachers felt the need for assistance.

To move from the demands of primary school teachers to those of secondary colleagues — the Schools Council 'Enquiry I' (1968) lists teachers' preferences for courses connected with ROSLA. Teachers asked to be told more about new developments in particular subjects, and about new techniques that they could use to put across the new curriculum to their pupils. They asked for discussions and conferences at which ideas could be 'pooled'. There were also requests from teachers who wanted to find out more about work in different fields of employment, and from those who wanted to attend social science courses, so that they could learn more about the background and behaviour of the fifteen plus age group.

Brian Cane's survey was carried out in Durham, Norfolk, and Glamorgan, and in each of these three counties, 80 per cent of the teachers expressed a need for in-service training. Of the courses designed to meet these needs, one hundred and fifty-nine were provided by the LEAs, forty by the universities, and seventy by other bodies. However, although the teachers showed a willingness to attend courses, and although many were provided by varying agencies:

> 'Only one in ten of the teachers, and a few of the heads, thought that courses were planned with the individual circumstances of teachers in mind'. (Cane, 1969)

The 1969 DES Survey also showed that it was not general for teachers to be able to attend courses of their own choosing. At that time there would seem to have been a communication gap, or a lack of understanding between the course providers and the teachers. With the consolidation of the teachers' centre network, and the strengthening of relationships, it is quite possible that these weaknesses have been somewhat alleviated in the last few years.

It should have been relatively easy to rectify a further fault highlighted by Brian Cane's research:

> '66 per cent of the teachers in all counties reported as their chief complaint that they were seldom or never told the degree of knowledge or skill required of an applicant for the course. In-service training provides for the experienced and inexperienced teacher, the highly qualified specialist and less knowledgeable colleagues'. (*ibid.*)

More careful planning and a greater clarification of objectives should make it possible for courses to be advertized accurately, so that applicants know for what they are volunteering. In some situations it is preferable to have a 'mixed ability group', but on many occasions, time and patience can be wasted when teachers of too wide an interest and experience range are summoned to a vaguely described meeting.

After his investigation into in-service provision in two local authorities, E. S. Henderson (1975) concluded that frustrations caused by attendance on courses that are too general may result in increased demands for school-based courses which have more limited objectives and clientéle.

Among the other findings of the DES Survey was the fact that only four per cent of the teaching force had been involved in the staffing of courses in the previous three years. This low percentage is interesting when we learn from research into in-service training in two counties, conducted by E. J. Hollick (1972), that in Hampshire 48 per cent and in Kent 42 per cent of teachers' centre courses in 1971 were staffed by serving teachers. Furthermore headteachers interviewed reported that there were other potential in-service training tutors on their staffs. One of Hollick's main findings was that in 1971, 35 per cent of the teacher applicants were failing to obtain a place on courses due to over subscription. Many conclusions could be drawn from this evidence, but it does seem that in these authorities that have a high level of teacher involvement in courses organized by teachers' centres, there is a correspondingly high level of teacher demand.

Even among the many far-reaching recommendations of the Plowden Report (DES, 1967), it was suggested that:

'Local centres are invaluable in supporting the innovations introduced by individual teachers, the source of most educational progress. They ought to start from a knowledge of what local teachers are doing. They can provide opportunities for teachers to meet others who are a little ahead of themselves but whose practice is within their reach.'

It seems that because the classroom teachers have direct contact with various problems and because they are not too distant from the attending teacher's own position, the activities they lead are well supported.

Despite this support, Brian Cane reported in 1969 that:

'The overall picture for the year 1966—7 is one of a general poverty of provision of courses by the three local authorities, in spite of the praise-worthy work of County Staffs, and the many interesting initiatives taken by the County authorities'. (Cane, *op. cit.*)

In the last ten years, in-service provision has increased enormously, but many teachers still fail to obtain places on the. courses of their choice, and they become used to receiving messages such as — 'I am sorry to inform you that Course X is over-subscribed — we will try to arrange a similar series at a future date'.

Where centres have been in existence for many years, as well as repeating activities to satisfy public demand their leaders often report that increased teacher involvement, improved channels of communication, and the building up of good personal relation-ships, has made the work more meaningful. As one warden explained at a Schools Council Regional Study Conference held at Matlock College of Education in 1972: 'Increasingly within the past two years, colleagues have expressed a desire to look at topics in greater depth, and there has been a swing away from "tips for teachers type sessions".' It seems likely that this 'swing' is facili-tated by the establishment of an adequately staffed teachers' centre, for courses held in varying venues may suffer through lack of local preparation and follow-up work. Not only can topics be covered in more depth where there has been a period of consolida-tion, but it seems that in some centres the nature of the courses is altered also. In an article titled 'Developing Teachers' Centres' (1972), Joslyn Owen described a centre, where over a five year period, it was possible to arrange meetings that gradually took in themes of concern to teachers of pupils in a broader age range, and where subject divisions began to be broken down.

Although some teachers' centres do attract equal support from primary and secondary schools, the following situation seems fairly common:

'A major problem for many centres was how to attract secondary teachers to their activities. Many reported that the vast majority of habitués were from primary schools, and this determined the emphasis in the programme of activities'. (Schools Council Pamphlet 6, 1970)

Secondary schools are often large enough to hold an even greater stock of resources than teachers' centres, and if necessary they can arrange their own in-service training. Furthermore, some secondary colleagues feel drawn to activities initiated by subject associations, university schools of education, and polytechnics. These and other factors have contributed to the evolution of teachers' centre programmes that frequently have a primary school bias.

Statistics from the DES Survey support the proposal that there is such a bias, but they also divide the 'clientele' into further categories:

'Of one hundred (*sic*) attenders at teachers' centres, approximately eighteen could be expected to be heads, ten deputies, twenty heads of departments, sixteen graded post holders, and thirty-two assistant teachers. About fifty-two came from the primary school sector of education, twenty from secondary modern schools, nine from grammar schools, thirteen from comprehensives, and other types of secondary schools and three from special schools'. (Townsend, 1970)

Teachers' centre attendance would seem to be related to seniority, as well as to type of school. More limited surveys carried out in Nottinghamshire (Bradley, Flood, Padfield, 1975) also showed that primary school teachers were more regular teachers' centre attenders than their secondary school counterparts and that heads and deputies were again particularly frequent visitors. This research also showed that probationers and those with twenty-one to thirty years experience were more likely to attend teachers' centres and that those with from eleven to twenty years experience were least likely.

One way in which centre attendance can be deliberately influenced, is by organizing more day-time courses during term time, so that headteachers can suggest to individual members of staff that they participate. It is possible that this 'semi-compulsory' attendance may 'uncover' an interest that might encourage more out of school involvement. From Brian Cane's research it is evident that teachers:

'would like the bulk of in-service training to take place close to their own school or home, preferably during school hours, but failing that, at a convenient starting time after school, for a half-day or full day at week-ends, or up to one full week during vacations'. (Cane, 1969)

In Harriet Townsend's DES Survey, school time was not surprisingly the most popular choice for course attendance, but even then, only 58 per cent were prepared to make use of the teachers' centre. Fifty-four per cent said they would use it immediately after school; 50 per cent said they would attend during the evening; 38 per cent said 'yes' to holiday use; and 24 per cent supported weekend attendance. As an addendum, between 22 per cent and 30 per cent expressed themselves neutral to all propositions. It is important to re-emphasize that the DES Survey was carried out ten years ago, when only 8.8 per cent of all courses were sited locally in teachers' centres. From a perusal of current teachers' centre programmes, 16.15, 16.30 and 16.45 seem to be popular starting times for meetings, although in some centres meetings held at 19.00, 19.30 and 20.00 hrs are becoming well favoured. The frequency of meetings held out of school hours may result from disquiet caused to teachers when their absence causes inconvenience to colleagues left in school.

In view of the present financial situation, and the problems caused by widespread cutbacks in staffing it is interesting to note that in Brian Cane's study —

'The most striking feature of the provision for training during 1966—7, was that none of the three authorities arranged any non-residential courses in the vacations, although the survey shows that such courses would command considerable support from teachers. Further, universities in the area provided few courses for local teachers during vacation time'. (*ibid.*)

As management in education and industry seeks ways of gaining greater financial return for investment, it would seem advisable to make greater use of teachers' centres during the vacations, so that teachers can attend courses at times when they are less harried by school pressures. In an attempt to up-date and localize the information obtained by Cane (1969) and Townsend (1970), C. A. Nichols and L. H. Weeks (1975) carried out a small-scale survey to research the needs of teachers in Berkshire and surrounding areas. From eighty-eight completed questionnaires, preferences for duration and location of courses were ascertained. For many types of course local centres and the college of education received roughly equal support, but in this survey more teachers preferred the college as a venue for courses in primary mathematics and the language arts. On the other hand more colleagues chose local centres as venue for courses on teaching socially handicapped and maladjusted children, and also primary science. In general the survey showed more teachers preferring to attend short courses in local centres, but one might also deduce that college of education tutorial expertise might sensibly be further utilized by taking some long award-bearing courses to teachers' centres in areas where a college is not easily accessible.

Despite the earlier references to teachers' preferences for times of course attendance, one of the major advantages of teachers' centres is that they give service and support at the time it is needed:

'In the daily task of teacher-pupil contact, a considerable proportion of teachers are using centres for enervation, and some are involved in genuine innovation. The essence of in-service opportunities at centres is the continual process that is available when an individual feels he needs it, rather than the provision of instant solutions'. (Beresford, 1974).

Nevertheless, it seems that when a district is in the throes of re-organization, such as that needed for the setting up of a comprehensive system, or when national attention is focussed on a problem, such as by the Bullock Report (DES, 1975) on the teaching of reading, then teachers are more prepared to enrol for in-service courses. It is when the events that disturb the *status quo* have passed that centres have to guard against apathy.

It may be that the pressures exerted by organizational change, and by the recommendations of national reports, shed light on two different approaches to in-service work which Michael Eraut has labelled the 'solution-centred approach' and the 'problem centred-approach' —

'In the solution-centred approach there is assumed to be a solution which fits a large number of teachers' problems, and the purpose of in-service training is to transmit it. Whereas in the problem-centred approach, the emphasis of in-service education is on diagnosis and discussion of possible solutions'. (Eraut, 1972).

The 'problem-centred approach' would seem to match the ethos of most teachers' centres more satisfactorily, especially as the emphasis of many Nuffield and other projects has been on practical problem solving, and this has influenced the nature of many teachers' centre activities —

'Teachers apparently find the least acceptable teaching method is the lecture series without discussion, because this is a method that denies to the teacher the opportunity of contributing his own experiences. It also prevents him from giving expression to those feelings of anxiety that are an occupational hazard in in-service education, concerned as it is mostly with disturbing change'. (Price, 1973)

Discussion and seminar groups, practical workshop activities, simulation exercises, and the open forum type of meeting fill a large part of many teachers' centre programmes, and an examination of these programmes reveals few lecture sessions without discussion.

In recent years there has been a trend towards not only basing in-service education in school premises, but on focussing the programme on the needs of a particular school or schools. This emphasis on school-focussed work has been especially important, because many organizers of in-service activities have been disappointed when ideas and practices introduced on courses have had little or no impact on the schools, because the one or two teachers attending have been unable to persuade other members of staff that the ideas and practices were worth acting upon. At the Sixth Annual Conference for Teachers' Centre Leaders held at Newcastle-upon-Tyne in 1976, wardens spent much of the time considering and discussing the problems connected with school-focussed work.

As yet the documentation of school focussed activities is very limited but papers such as that written by Del Goddard (1976), which describes in detail a Language Policy Project at a boys' comprehensive school does suggest ways in which development for a more restricted clientele can be fostered. Dr Patricia Ashton and her team were also concerned with the needs of whole staffs when they devised the course material which follows up the Schools Council 'Aims of Primary Education' project. Material contained in the associated publication *Aims into Practice in the Primary School* (Ashton *et al.*, 1975), depends for its success on the headteachers attending externally based meetings, returning to their schools and using the same material with their whole staff.

b) As centres for curriculum development

'Although it may be said that in-service education is, in general, passive and requires in-puts, whereas curriculum development is dynamic and creates out-puts, in practice the two are often closely related. For example, teachers who discuss, examine and modify materials for teaching are certainly combining the two'. (Culling, 1974)

These words of George Culling provide a reinforced link between this and the previous section. They remind us of the dependence of one activity on the other, although many practising in-service education tutors would challenge the claim that their service is 'in general passive'. Despite this reservation it seems that where teachers' centres are deeply involved in curriculum development there is a considerable degree of dynamism, and a fair number of outputs. An additional link between curriculum development and in-service education is that the latter becomes necessary when curriculum development has met with success, that can be shared by more colleagues in more schools.

Curriculum development will vary according to the nature of the situation for which the new curriculum is planned. However, in most cases it can be described as —

'defining the aims and objectives of teaching, constructing appropriate methods and materials, assessing their effectiveness, and feeding back the result of their use, to provide a starting point for a further cycle'. (*ibid.*)

For the teachers' centre personnel there seems to be a need to help plan the establishment of objectives to help organize the methods and materials, to help teachers find ways of motivating the pupils who are exposed to the new curriculum, and then help with the evaluation of the whole project.

Through teachers' centres colleagues are involved in both national and local curriculum development. National curriculum development is frequently connected with bodies such as the Schools Council and the NFER, and so will be described in Chapter 5. However, curriculum interest in national projects can be generated either from the centre, or from the 'grass roots'. For instance, some teachers' centres have been involved in the Schools Council 'Geography for the Young School Leaver' Project, because of LEA cooperation with the Project team, while some are now involved because the published materials have attracted the interest of local teachers.

Group organization for curriculum development is less straight-forward than for its in-service training parallels. Curriculum development may involve no more than one teacher at the initial stages, for some planning, devising and testing is carried out by an individual teacher, and then the work is made available for wider consideration. For example, one teacher used a teachers' centre as a base for his work on a natural history project, and then invited interested teachers to evaluate and improve the material. In this case the centre staff were able to help with reference, reprographic and audiovisual support, and by acting as a link between the 'developer' and other teachers. Besides development that is accomplished by teachers who set out on their own, curriculum work is carried out by study groups, working parties, teachers' workshops, and sub-committees.

In a 1975 article, Mr Tony Light, formerly Joint Secretary of the Schools Council, described three models for curriculum development. His first is the 'Intervention Model' where outside experts diagnose the problem, suggest the cure, and the teacher is expected to 'administer the dose'. His second type is called 'the independence model' where a school attempts to devise a solution without regard for the experiences of others. Mr Light says that when this happens:

'many teachers' energies are spent in duplicating materials such as local archives that already exist in comparable form else-where, and could be more efficiently produced centrally'.

His third type is called 'the cooperative model' and where this is in operation, teachers work with outside consultants to develop schemes that although geared for a particular school or group of schools, are nonetheless influenced by the experience of those who have already experimented in similar projects. Despite the Englishman's traditional independence it would seem that Mr Light's third model is the one that has most to commend it.

Even though 'the cooperative model' has been praised, it is important to re-assert the individual teachers' place in the centre of the innovative process. Cooperation is commended as an acknowledgement of the contribution that can be made by a team supported by specialists, and not because the teachers feel the need for direction. For with a centre of their own —

'teachers have felt they were on neutral ground, without hierarchical control and able to carry out programmes of curriculum development based on their own practical experience and matched to their classroom needs'. (Wright, 1974)

An example of this type of development emanating from a teachers' centre, is a foreign language scheme for less able fourteen- and sixteen-year-olds, that was devised by a small group of teachers who, having found a classroom need, carried out their work from the teachers' centre. The group sought advice from the local School of Educational Studies, the LEA provided some financial assistance, the Schools Council through its Field Officer gave the group a much needed morale booster and through the Morrell Fund some much needed money, and the teachers' centre leader provided them with technological resources. Their material was tested in local schools, and is now being more widely produced so that teachers from a greater number of schools can make use of it if they so wish.

The subject area in which local curriculum development work is most widespread and most eagerly adopted is that connected with local studies. As schools base more of their work on a study of the immediate environment, and on direct experience, so has the need for information and materials become more urgent. Beside the pressures caused by changes in educational philosophy, innovation has been hastened by the fact that there is generally a dearth of materials on strictly local topics. Whereas it is commercially viable for a publisher to invest in a general book on farm buildings, it is unlikely that there would be a widespread demand for a booklet produced to help teachers and children, when a parti-

cular medieval barn in Long Newnton, Gloucestershire was being
visited.

Interested observers of local curriculum development are
frequently only made aware of completed products, whether they
are available in book, broadcast, or multi-media format. Because
of this, a short paper written by John Hilsum (1976), describing
the processes leading to the production of a local history pack on
'Victoria's Island' makes enlightening reading. Mr Hilsum
describes the composition of the curriculum group, the collection
of the materials, the clarification of aims and objectives, and the
evaluation, production and dissemination of the completed
resources. The blueprint of educational objectives under eight
headings, with the opportunity to record critical incidence is
particularly noteworthy, but Mr Hilsum has to admit that he has
not been tempted to repeat such an 'elaborate technique'.

Teachers' centre leaders and teachers who are experienced in
curriculum development work stress the importance of making
sure that early sorties in this field have a good chance of success:

> 'any professional centre's first development scheme must be,
> and be seen to be successful. The scheme need not be large, but it
> must deal with a real and urgent issue facing a definable group
> of teachers in the area'. (Rudd in Watkins (ed), 1973)

In addition, the other teachers in the area need to be kept informed
of the group's progress and achievements. In this way, the centre's
'parish' feels involved in the work of a range of study groups, so
that the claim — 'Curriculum development is only for the golden'
cannot be substantiated. (Greenwood, in Thornbury (ed), 1973)

In the conclusions of the 1972 NUT Survey of Teachers'
Centres, the compilers remind us that:

> 'One reason for the establishment of teachers' centres was to
> enable programmes of curriculum development to be
> developed. Some centres and authorities were criticised in the
> survey, for little or no involvement in this field',

Although the survey carries limited weight because of the low
return rate of questionnaires (35 per cent), it does remind us, that
despite Schools Council exhortations, and the dreams of many

idealists there is still much to be done to promote development that strikes at the heart of the curriculum.

Despite the above reservations, it is possible that many teachers' centres are being forced, or are choosing to do more than their manpower and material resources permit. In centres that have large staffs, like the one in the south with a staff of eighteen, or in centres that were connected to a major scheme, such as the North West Regional Development Project, it seems that progress can be made. Fifteen local centres are linked through the University of Manchester School of Education in the North West Project, and teams of teachers have worked to produce materials for the 'early leaving' fourth and fifth year pupils. Teacher and pupil materials in the following subject areas have been prepared — English, Domestic Science, Social Education, Music and Team Teaching.

The North West Regional Project has shown what can be achieved when curriculum development is given generous financial support, and when teacher involvement is highly organized. Local teachers' centres will always have a special duty to produce local studies materials, but some teachers may have acquired the notion that curriculum development is merely concerned with the production of this type of work. Because of this, support such as was given to the North West Project should be extended so that suggestions still in the 'thought and talk' stage can be fully developed. Maybe then it will be possible to agree with Ronald Cave who in 1971 claimed that 'both the quality and the quantity of the present enthusiasm for reform based on development work is unmatched in our history of compulsory education'.

c) As resources centres

At the beginning of this section we should remind ourselves of the connection between resources and the other roles of teachers' centres already discussed. A resources centre that exists solely as a store of educational material and equipment may merely aim to supply the demands made on it. On the other hand a resources centre which is part of a multi-purpose teachers' centre needs to combine with the other functions to make the joint force of the establishment even more powerful.

If and when curriculum development groups reach the stage of producing teaching and learning materials, frustration can be caused if no way is found to produce what is needed. Some groups may find what they need on the commercial market, but for those who need to make new materials it is helpful if the centre can provide the necessary expertise, and hard and soft-ware. With the help of offset litho machines, electronic stencil-cutters, photo-copiers, ink and spirit duplicators etc. teachers are able to produce their own paper materials. Armed with audio and videotape and cassette recorders, they can record and play back their own sounds and pictures. Using transparency makers, still and cine cameras, and TV cameras they can make some of the necessary visual materials.

As well as providing the resources for curriculum development groups, teachers' centres also provide services that support in-service training programmes —

'tape recording facilities, reprographic facilities, workshop facilities, and so forth . . . are the kinds of support that the centre must offer in order to prevent the ideas from sinking into the ground'. (Davidson in Childs *et al.*, 1972)

A perusal of some current teachers' centre programmes reveals details of courses such as 'Audio-Visual Aids Equipment Work-shop', 'The First and Middle Schools Resources Centre', 'Photo-graphy and Photocopying', 'The applications of Closed Circuit TV'. It is not possible or desirable for every school to equip itself with every new piece of equipment, but many teachers' centres are trying to enlarge their facilites so that the in-service encourage-ment to experiment with new materials and machines, need not be left to 'sink into the ground'.

When centre leaders are canvassing to promote increased use of the centres, they find that some teachers are not keen to attend in-service courses, or support curriculum development work. However, they may be pleased, for example, to borrow a film, or use the stencil-cutter. Visits made in connection with resources may persuade them that the centre has something to offer, and at a latter date they may feel more inclined to participate in some of the centre activities.

Desirable though many of these resources may be, they are of no use unless systematically organized, and efficiently maintained. Many small teachers' centres are at a disadvantage because they do not have the essential 'back-up' staff to provide an adequate service. Larger centres often employ a team of ancillary helpers who work where support is needed. In many cases these helpers are well trained and qualified, and are able to make available to teachers a particularly valuable resource — *time*. At one centre a teachers' typist has been appointed, and she is able to service the groups who are working in different areas of the curriculum.

At another centre —

'One of the most useful services that we offer is a teachers' workshop, and again this involves employing people, in this case two very highly skilled technicians whom you can go to in order to have some very quick assistance to develop some ideas, that you want to get cracking within the school'. (*ibid.*)

Where workshop technicians are able to help teachers make equipment, and apparatus according to plans drawn up by teachers, a considerable financial saving can be achieved. At one centre the technician produced chart storage units and other pieces of furniture for nearly all the schools in the area. Consequently, although schools pay for material used, they can take advantage of money saved through the use of this service. To the same ends, where no other central organization exists, some teachers' centres buy in cine films, framed pictures, tape recordings etc, and make them available for loan. Now that large comprehensive schools are able to invest in expensive equipment, teachers' centre provision can be overtaken, but there are still many small and average sized schools that can benefit considerably from a 'pooling' of resources at the centres.

However it is not realistic for teachers' centres to accommodate a fully comprehensive range of resource material and equipment, and for this reason many leaders try to keep a record on paper, or in their heads, of where further resources can be located:

'a request for a dozen African horned toads was not met by extracting them from a store-cupboard in the centre, but by arranging contact with the science department in a school and a college'. (Beresford, 1974)

Centre leaders who are able to direct teachers to the resources that they need, are likely to enlist the support and gratitude of their clientele.

On a wider scale, one county has pioneered a system in which several teachers' centres, and a   central resource centre are coordinated to make up a network of resource providers. Chapter 5 Section (b), contains details of an even more ambitious scheme, in which a charitable foundation, a public company, several teachers' centres and a university have all cooperated to make a regional resources centre a success.

In Inner London, a team of media resources officers have been added to the establishments of teachers' centres. These officers are specially trained in information retrieval, CCTV, photography, graphics, reprographics, and sound recording. Furthermore in 1972 a large media resources centre was opened in London, and there teachers are able to learn about and use highly specialized audiovisual aids, and to have mass-produced the teaching materials that they have devised. This centre has since become part of the ILEA Learning Materials Service.

Until now it would seem that the development of teachers' centres as resource centres has depended on the existing level of provision from other sources. Most LEA libraries and museum services are often well operated and stocked, and so it is in the educational technology department, and in the local materials field that teachers' centres have been able to provide services which do not already exist.

d) As information providers

In recent years there has been a huge increase in the amount of available information connected with education. Public libraries and university education libraries continue to be the main sources of 'book information', but for many teachers their local teachers' centre seems to be the place to turn to for information connected with their profession.

The most obvious example of information provided by the centres are the details of its own programme, and the facilities that it can provide. News from the centres is distributed weekly, fortnightly, monthly, bi-termly, termly or haphazardly, and centre circulars range from duplicated sheets to professionally produced posters and handbooks. Newsletters often accompany course details, and these act as a more personal bridge between the centres and the schools.

Most centre news is relayed through the post, but teachers' centre leaders, like many other communicators are finding that paper 'hand-outs' are too easily ignored or forgotten. Consequently, some centres are broadcasting their news over local radio networks. One local radio station allocates daily a five minute section to local educational matters, and the teachers' centre publicizes its activities during this time. The use of this medium not only focusses teacher interest on centre activities, but also makes the general public more aware of educational matters.

In a much less public way, centre leaders use the display and exhibition areas of the centres to draw attention to a wide variety of topics. Notice-boards give news of coming centre events, details of curriculum development projects, and of meetings to be held at other venues. Centres are also on the mailing lists of many associations and organizations and their literature can generally be referred to.

Centres that have suitable accommodation, arrange exhibitions of educational equipment and publications, and of work done by children and teachers. Through the latter, teachers are able to learn about subjects other than those in which they have been personally involved. One centre leader arranges between eighty and ninety commercial exhibitions each year, and in most centres, teachers are given opportunities to find out about manufacturers' products by examining their wares.

Postal communications, local radio broadcasts, and exhibitions of various kinds, all provide teachers with assorted information, but teachers' centres seem to be sources of more informally requested information as well. For if a teacher asks 'How can I stick two polythene bags together?', or 'Where can I find out more about dyslexia?', or 'Where can I observe the Audio-Page machine in use?', an immediate answer is generally expected. Of course it is impossible for the staff of any one centre to have ready-made answers to every request, but in time it should be possible to collect sources of information, and the addresses of people to whom a follow-up to an increasing array of queries can be made.

Many centres do not limit their provision of information to the educational, and this advertisement from a Camden Westminster Teachers' Centre Newsletter (1974) exemplifies a more general service —

'If you have anything to exchange?
flats, equipment, furniture,
or to sell:
car, bike, books, clothes,

Why not use our unique facility?
No charge
Wide circulation

It may well be that domestic help of this nature can make it possible for teachers to cope with their classroom responsibilities more calmly.

More directly connected with teaching is the bulletin produced by one centre, that provides information on all the educational and related services that are provided in the district. Such a readily available source book must be invaluable, especially to colleagues who are new to the area. In a more specific way, directories of local school journey destinations, produced by some centres should make planning more efficient, and open up more possibilities for local studies.

When the subject of teachers' centres as providers of information is being considered, it is tempting to speculate as to where the information would be obtained were there no centre. Administrative offices would seem a possibility, but although factual information about school organization is easily acquired from this source, many teacher requests would seem to be more naturally dealt with by personnel, whose first concern is with decision making directly connected with the curriculum.

e) As social centres for teachers

Bearing in mind the Englishman's love of a cup of tea, we should not be surprised to read that — 'All that can safely be said of every teachers' centre in the country is that it has a tea-making capacity' (Stevens, 1971). Many teachers' centre meetings take place immediately the school day has ended, so a pause for tea between the rush to the centre and the start of a session often provides badly needed refreshment. In addition, because teachers converge on the centre from many different schools, there is a need for socializing to be made easy, and a cup of tea seems to 'lubricate' conversation!

Teachers' social needs vary enormously, but it seems that younger colleagues may be the ones most in need of 'a place to go for company'. Having left behind them the communal life of colleges and universities, they may be pleased to meet together in a relaxed atmosphere away from school. In addition:

'young teachers fresh out of college may well feel they have had more than their fair share of discussion and debate in the preceding three or four years, but would be happy to attend centres for social purposes, especially if they are living and teaching in rather isolated areas'. (Cave, 1971)

Teaching can be a very lonely profession, and teachers' centres meet some social needs, especially for newly qualified teachers, and for newcomers to the area.

The extent of social activities is already quite considerable in some centres. For example, one city centre is open for Club Night every Monday and Thursday, and in one summer term a Folk Evening, Discotheque, Ceilidh, Car Rally, and Party were organized. Another centre seems to have an even more lively social set-up —

'My own centre stays open until 23.30 because we have a fully fledged bar that is open five evenings a week, and on the social side we have social activities that go on every night until 23.00, and sometimes on Friday till 01.00 hours'. (Hutchins in Childs *et al.*, 1972)

However some leaders see no reason why they should be concerned with social events, while they are hard-pressed to fulfil their educational objectives, and the surveys of Bradley, Flood and Padfield (1975) showed that there was a lack of enthusiasm for social activities based at the centres in question. Nevertheless, a teacher who is helped to relax and enjoy his leisure time through teacher centre provision may be able to fulfil his classroom and curriculum duties with more likelihood of success.

f) As centres for community involvement

In Victorian times, when Pupil-Teacher Centres played a part in the preparation of teachers, most schooling took place in establishments cut off from the surrounding community by high brick walls. Some divisions between parents and teachers and between schools and communities still exist, but in recent times there has been an erosion of many of these barriers. Encouraged by the research of educational sociologists, teachers have endeavoured to find out more about the pupil's home background, and educational authorities have financed 'community schools' and community centres within school campuses. Teachers' centres have also been influenced by this development and their programmes often reflect the needs of the surrounding district. In addition, many teachers try to become better acquainted with the area in which they are situated, for as one warden explained at the Schools Council Regional Conference held at Rutherford College, Canterbury in 1972: 'I think to work effectively in curriculum development as a warden of a centre it is vital to get to know your area in depth, and *NOT* just the schools, but the community as a whole'.

As centre organizers have concerned themselves with the surrounding neighbourhood, and as their participating teachers have become more involved with community needs, it has become necessary to increase liaison with other agencies concerned with young people. Once this liaison has been fostered, the centres have sometimes become the meeting places for non-teacher groups:

'Although ours is primarily a teachers' centre, there are other professions whose work, like ours, is with children and young people. On suitable occasions we have welcomed youth officers, social workers, industrial training officers, school secretaries, local historians — and even children'. (Gough in Thornbury (ed), 1973)

Provided areas like curriculum development do not suffer, it is certainly advantageous for teachers to mix with colleagues who serve the community in fields other than education.

Besides 'opening the doors' to a wider clientele, some teachers' centres are now welcoming parents to their activities — 'Increasingly parents are being drawn into the actual work of the centres — even larger numbers attend to see exhibitions of work'. (Cave, *op. cit.*) Such visits should initially make more parents aware of what is going on, not just in the schools at which their own children are pupils, but also give them greater insight into the varying approaches to education that exist within a small area. Increased insight may lead to greater understanding, which in turn may enable them to make a more enlightened contribution to the advancement of education for which teachers' centres are striving.

Chapter 5

Teachers' Centre Links with —

a) The LEA Advisory Services

In spite of the success of the Advisory Centre for Teachers at the University of London Institute of Education, the Centre for the Teaching of Reading attached to Reading University School of Education, and the jointly sponsored Centre at the University of Surrey, these centres are not typical, for the majority of teachers' centres operate under the auspices of the local education authorities. The main explanation for this is that the universities were generally slow to implement the McNair Report's recommendations, and the centres connected with the Nuffield Maths and Science projects were so successful that multi-purpose centres grew from these project-orientated beginnings.

Because curriculum schemes such as the Nuffield Maths Project had to be locally organized, it was to be expected that chief education officers would often delegate this responsibility to their advisory teams, which have expanded rapidly during the last seventeen years. Such organization, though necessary, has sometimes left a tradition of advisory involvement that is out of keeping with recommendations such as those by the Schools Council which has championed the cause of teacher-initiated activities.

Just as teachers' centres are characterized by their lack of uniformity, so is there great variety in the degree of advisory involvement in the organization of activities at teachers' centres. Some centres are led by members of the advisory staff, others have programmes that are dominated by advisers, others never include items in their programme without the 'blessing' of a member of the advisory team, some have their links through an adviser who represents the Authority on the teachers' centre committee, others only have contact with advisers when the teachers' centre leader needs help, and some centres have no links whatsoever with the advisory teams.

This variety is illustrated by examples of the differing ways advisers are involved in teachers' centre committee organization. The constitution of one centre management committee designates a place for the senior schools adviser or a person nominated by him; the constitution of another centre merely says that members of the advisory team may attend consultative committee meetings if they wish; the constitution of a further centre committee allows no advisory voice to be heard. However, teachers' centre committee structure is part of the more formal organization, and advisory influence is often exerted, for good or ill, at the informal level of operations.

At the root of some of the problems that exist between centres and LEA advisers is the lack of role definition for the adviser and the teachers' centre leader. The advisers have inherited some of the more forbidding characteristics of members of Her Majesty's Inspectorate, and this inheritance is not helped by calling some LEA advisers, inspectors. Although the title inspector may put teachers on their guard, the word adviser also causes some misunderstanding. Is their main responsibility to advise the teacher, or is it to advise the education officers, or is it to advise both? Added to this confusion is the uncertainty of role definition of advisory teachers, who often perform the same task as advisers, but who are generally more distant from policy-making decisions.

In *The Management of Curriculum Development* Joslyn Owen (1973) reported that — 'The degree to which advisers are asked to support the warden and secretaries of centres, varies almost whimsically'. — but perhaps this is just as well, because of the differing ways advisers approach their job —

'At this stage, the trustworthy, sound, hardworking and humane helper will be relied upon. But the adviser who still thinks in terms of inspection and of old-established statuses will be of little use'. (*ibid.*)

When advisory and centre staff, and local teachers were involved in absorbing schemes, such as the preparation of the Nuffield Mathematics and Science 5—13 materials, problems of hierarchical and role differences disappeared, so it is to be hoped that similar priority participation will 'weld' the would-be partners together.

Many centre leaders have realized that advisers have an important part to play in curriculum development, for as an East Midlands warden said at the second National Conference of Wardens:

> 'They are aware of school developments and needs, have a particular subject or curriculum area specialism for developments, and if there is a partnership in a centre then they should be very much involved'. (North and East Midlands Wardens, 1972)

Even if centre leaders are able to become involved in the work of the surrounding schools, they will still be more limited in their experiences and observations, especially as advisers are likely to represent the LEA at regional, national, and sometimes international conferences. In many areas, advisers prevent the centres becoming too 'parochial', by transmitting news from other schools and establishments.

Despite the fact that LEA advisers can make a distinctive contribution to teachers' centre developments, at the Schools Council Conference on 'Teachers' Centres and the Developing Curriculum' held at St Osyth's College of Education, Clacton in 1972, one speaker declared that —

> 'the adviser and the teachers' centre warden do exactly the *same job*. . . . The warden is a curriculum adviser as far as I am concerned, and should be seen to be functioning as such'.

The most debatable words in these sentences are 'exactly the same job' for although advisers, and teachers' centre leaders can often be seen performing the same function, different weight can be attached to their authority, because the teacher centre leader has 'no axe to grind'. He is emphatically an agent of the teachers as well as the LEA, and as such he can give advice as an equal colleague, in the knowledge that that advice does not have to be part of some collective policy. Additionally, a teachers' centre leader is only concerned with appointments within his centre whereas most advisers are involved in staff appointments especially with promotions. It is this involvement that may sometimes inhibit teachers when advisers are present at teachers' centre activities. Besides, some teachers may be tempted to follow an adviser's lead, not because of sincerely held convictions, but because they wish to impress those concerned with promotion decisions.

Although authoritarianism may have no place, it seems appropriate that advisers should be able to use teachers' centre premises as bases for their supportive functions. For whilst teachers' centre wardens have accommodation that is suitable for a wide variety of activities, participation in teachers' centre activities can also make advisers more accessible, and this is important since the effects of local government re-organization have in some areas made schools feel more isolated.

It seems that the most satisfactory arrangement exists when a balance is achieved whereby advisers feel welcome when arranging courses and meetings at teachers' centres, and where they take an interest in the general well-being of the centre without trying to dominate or dictate. Unfortunately, in spite of the Wardens in the South East's (WISE) early dictum that the Centres should be — 'Of the Teachers, Governed by the Teachers, and for the Teachers', in 1970 Michael Pollard claimed that —

'So far from being places of the teachers' own, many teachers' centres have been virtually taken over by the LEA inspectorate, without whose permission neither the warden nor the committee of teacher stool-pigeons dare to make a move'.

This state of affairs probably exists where teachers' centre leaders are too overworked or too weak to provide adequate leadership, where teachers have been reluctant to take initiative themselves, or where there has been an inadequate consideration of objectives and strategic planning.

Where advisers do exert undue pressure on teachers' centres it is likely to be in a far more specialist area than that influenced by the centre leaders. For whereas leaders of multi-purpose centres endeavour to coordinate activities that cover all subjects for all age groups, advisers generally have a subject or age group brief, and so through specialist courses the curriculum can become too segmented. Nevertheless just because some course provision has been short-sighted, teachers' centre leaders would be unwise to refuse the help of specialists, for in that way mediocrity is tolerated.

One of the basic problems connected with advisory links with teachers' centres is the degree of independence that should be vested in the centre. Where centre leaders act on the recommendations of the Management/Consultative/Advisory Committees, conflict can arise when teachers ask for courses that are 'out of step' with advisory policy. For instance teachers may ask for a course on 'Teaching Modern Languages to Mixed Ability Groups' while it may be advisory policy only to teach languages to the more able. Some centre leaders hold fast to the principle of autonomy, and arrange activities regardless of any conflict that may arise. By this action teachers are being allowed academic freedom, and the right to make choices according to their own professional discretion. On the other hand some centre leaders try not to confuse teachers by exposing them to approaches that are contradictory or incompatible. There are dangers in the second policy, but whichever course is taken the need for more consultation, and cooperation becomes daily more apparent for as Geoffrey Mattock reports in Watkins (ed), 1973), the situation is far from straightforward:

'Whilst the chief-inspector or senior-adviser, if an authority has one, is responsible for the policy of the advisory staff, teachers' centres often operate quite separately and without much reference to the advisory staff. Add to this, the further complication that finance, release of teachers, grants, etc. are usually dealt with by the FE administration and a somewhat complex situation is apparent'.

In some authorities, one adviser has the task of coordinating in-service education, and through his work, unnecessary duplication and mismanagement can be avoided. In addition some LEAs have made appointments that may give the advisory service a less authoritarian role. They have appointed curriculum development advisers, who have no part in the assessment of teachers. These appointments could be undesirable, if curriculum development became the sole 'province' of an individual adviser, but if the activity is given more encouragement, and even more advisers are to be without 'subject labels', then the teachers' centre advisory links could be strengthened.

One of the advantages of having strong links between teachers' centres and advisory teachers is that these teachers, who have few administrative encumbrances can act as a link between the centre and the classrooms. Advisory teachers who tutor in-service courses, or who chair curriculum development groups can work alongside the participating teachers when they return to the classroom. Some wardens of teachers' centres also act as advisory teachers, and as such they often have access to finance which can be used to support the schools who need classroom equipment to put teachers' centre suggestions into practice.

In one teachers' centre programme, there are details of a course in which six advisory teachers were to act as a team in the development of a theme that could be approached in an integrated way. The advisory teachers specialize in environmental studies, art and craft, music, PE, science and the language arts. Because these teachers could follow-up the course individually or in groups it seems likely that the teachers would not have any enthusiasm blunted through lack of 'after care'.

The above example of an interdisciplinary approach is interesting in that it would only be possible in a multi-purpose teachers' centre, for some of the more recently established centres have been set aside for special subject work. Where we have, for example, history and social studies teachers' centres, local centres for English, a housecraft centre, music centres, and a centre for urban educational studies, it is possible for the 'curriculum development to be directly controlled by the LEA advisers, or inspectorate who may or may not consult teachers in determining the programme'. (Thornbury, 1973)

As the number of teachers' centres has grown, and as they have become more widely recognized as having a contribution to make by a greater proportion of educational opinion, the leaders of teachers' centres are increasingly making their viewpoint known especially now that most are now organized into associations. Through these associations, possible rifts between centre leaders and advisers may be enlarged, but in-service education and curriculum development depends so much on cooperation, that time spent on status-hunting and competition for teacher support would seem wasteful, especially as in the words of Joslyn Owen (1973):

> 'There is little to be said about the present state of participation of both types of inspectorate in local curriculum development work other than to say that less than what is possible seems to be achieved'.

b) Colleges and departments of education
Following the recommendation of McNair —

> 'We are convinced, however, it is the university, and no other body which must be the focus of the education and training of teachers in the future'. (Board of Education, 1944)

— the validation of teacher education and training was placed in the hands of the schools of education based at universities, and the coordination of in-service education was made the responsibility of the area training organization. Taking the advice of their training committees, consisting of university, college of education, LEA, DES, and teacher representatives, appointed tutors with administrative staff have organized programmes of courses and conferences for teachers from all types of schools.

Just as variety is a characteristic of teachers' centres, and of LEA involvement in their activities, so can variety be found in links between teachers' centres and ATOs. Some of the differences can be attributed to the geographical make-up of the organizations. Not only is it possible for a college of education to be under the auspices of a school of education that is in a quite different area, but ATOs coordinate in-service activities that cut across LEA boundaries. One of the strengths of this system has been that ATO committees have been able to provide programmes that have not been hidebound by local idiosyncracies.

Although members of training committees have regularly reported the needs of the schools to the course providers, 'as a result of discussion between Warden and ATO administrators, teacher opinion is now a greater factor than ever before'. (Schools Council Regional Study Conference, 4—7 June 1972) At one teachers' centre, the following school of education activities were included in the programme for one term — 'Young Teachers' Discussion Group', 'Introduction to Archaeology Course', 'Music for the Non-Music Specialist', 'Teaching in First Schools Course', and 'Trends in RE for the Seventies'.

School and Department of Education cooperation is particularly helpful to teachers' centres in providing links with university expertise, and sources of excellence from further afield. Links between the teachers' centres and the ATOs are also fruitful when they make it possible for conferences that have a wide appeal to be followed by local meetings at the centres. ATO provision is also helpful to teachers' centres, when meetings to consider several national projects can be arranged.

In 1969, a new departure in in-service education was announced by the DES. Through DES and LEA funds, and ATO organization, courses with a new format and with about sixty hours of teacher tutor contact time were to be arranged. The basic pattern for these courses has been an initial full-time period, of from two to seven days, which are usually residential, followed by regular part-time meetings held over one or two terms, and then a concluding full-time period of between one and five days. The regular part-time meetings are often accommodated at teachers' centres, because part of the ATO/DES policy is that the intermediate meetings should be occasions when colleagues from a more restricted area can give each other mutual support, especially where the course themes have local relevance. In 1971 Auriol Stevens reported that:

> 'In Devonshire the joint courses for in-service training of the ATOs and DES are being used by the LEA to pump money into the centres, and to ensure an academic standard which it is felt they might otherwise lack'.

By providing courses that have regional relevance, and then localizing the group work, this scheme has shown that national, regional, and local needs can be simultaneously taken into account.

University staff may be invited by teachers' centre leaders to act as consultants to curriculum development groups, or to help evaluate the work, or to advise where research is involved. Schools of education have also arranged courses for wardens on the leadership of groups. While frequently providing support, schools of education are loath to interfere —

'It was strongly emphasized that whilst the school of education was eager to help, it did not propose to direct the work . . . . the kind of help needed would be asked for by teachers, and it would arise out of their own thinking and work'. (Schools Council Pamphlet 3, 1969)

The North West Regional Project deserves a further mention at this point, because of the close links between the ATO and the teachers' centres that have been formed by involvement in the work. Although the project has received financial support from the Schools Council, it was initiated by the Manchester ATO who sent to the secondary schools in Manchester, a circular entitled, 'Forward from Newsom — a call to action'. The work that followed the answering of this call has had a great influence on the implementation of the ROSLA measures, and the university — LEA — centre cooperation that it has engendered, seems bound to influence future regional organization.

A rather different form of regional cooperation can be seen in the organization of the Regional Resources Centre, which is based at the University of Exeter. With funds made available through the Gulbenkian Foundation, and latterly through Philips Electrical Ltd., and through the coordination of the Exeter ATO, schools in a wide area can use the Centre which offers a vast range of technical facilities and expertise. Teachers needing to use the Centre make their inquiry through their own local teachers' centre.

The Exeter Regional Resources Centre is associated with the School of Education Library, and this cooperation reminds us of one of the most valuable links between the ATOs and teachers' centres. In addition to encouraging teachers to make use of the extensive facilities of education libraries, teachers' centres are able to borrow sets of books that act as support material for courses, and to use the information service that most of these libraries provide. From its inception the Centre for the Teaching of Reading set up by the School of Education at Reading University has given great encouragement to teachers and to multi-purpose local teachers' centres. Through its loan service, its course provision, and its publications, many teachers' centre leaders have become better equipped to meet the needs of teachers of 'A Language for Life'. In one of its many publications (Goodacre, 1975) teachers' centre provision for Reading is appraised and a Directory of Reading Centres is listed. It is probable that the publication of this booklet together with the recommendations of the Bullock Report (DES, 1975) encouraged many teachers' centres to improve their support for this area of the curriculum. The Centre at Reading provides an additional service through which school-based in-service work can be facilitated. Through the provision of cassette recordings and slide-tape sequences made by specialists on a wide range of language arts topics it is now possible for a whole staff to follow up teachers' centre activities by listening to and discussing the recorded talks in their own school situation.

One of the main ways in which colleges of education have been linked with teachers' centres, has been through ATO provision of in-service training opportunities. Having been asked by a centre leader for help with a course on a particular topic, the ATO tutor has often called upon college of education personnel to staff the courses. Alternatively, a centre leader may himself invite a college lecturer to lead a session, or a series of meetings. Similarly, there are times when groups working at teachers' centres need help with the evaluation of their work, and college staff may be called upon to do this.

Some teachers' centres have made provision for a college to be represented on their committee. However, as yet such representation is not widespread, and often depends on whether a college and centre are in close proximity. Distance also influences the extent to which college students are introduced to teachers' centres before their initial training is complete. In some areas, students on teaching practice in local schools are encouraged to use centre facilities for the preparation of teaching aids, and some colleges programme a visit to a teachers' centre before the students leave, so that they are familiar with the idea when they take up their first teaching appointments.

When a major curriculum project is based at a college of education, tutors, students, centre staff and local teachers have a common challenge, and may work together to forward the progress of the project. Colleagues involved with the Science Integrated Studies Project report that through teaching practice all parties have worked cooperatively with the trial materials, so that interest is kindled in readiness for in-service opportunities based at the teachers' centres.

Some centres are spared the friction that frequently exists when centre leaders are afraid that their work will be taken over by the colleges, or where college lecturers resent initiatives taken by centre leaders, simply because they are incorporated within a college of education. At one such centre, the leader has a joint appointment, spending half his time on centre duties, and half on college lecturing. Likewise, the media resources officer has a joint appointment. Schools Council Working Paper 10 recommended that teachers' centres should be set up in colleges, so, despite reservations from some centre leaders who fear the development of centres that have little independence, it is interesting to know that such centres can meet with success.

In the Sixties when teachers' centres were 'blossoming almost over night', the colleges of education were grappling with problems caused by the introduction of degree courses, and the extension of their premises to accommodate the massive increase in their student intake. Furthermore, the emphasis on 'grassroots' teacher involvement that had made university staff reluctant to intrude, may also have discouraged college staff from showing too much interest. This hesitancy may have been beneficial, in so far as it has allowed the centres to build a reputation for themselves, but maybe now is the time for such cooperation that has developed to be fostered for the mutual benefit of all.

The question of such cooperation has been considered in detail by a Working Party set up in 1975 by the Induction and In-Service Training Sub-Committee of the Advisory Committee on the Supply and Training of Teachers. The Working Party's report which is called 'The Contribution of Colleges and Departments of Education to INSET' has been sent to the Secretary of State for urgent consideration. The report contains a description of the opportunities presented by the availability of colleagues from the teacher education service for INSET, makes suggestions for the capitalization of this 'man-power' bonanza, and proposes organizational structures that facilitate deployment of 'appropriate tutors on a full-time or part-time basis for work of all kinds with colleagues in schools and teachers' centres'. The amount of this 'work of all kinds' would seem to be enormous, but a key word used in this suggestion is 'appropriate', for it would be unfortunate if tutors were 'put out in the field' *merely* because of the contraction of initial teacher education. Tutors from colleges and departments of education have for many years been constructively involved in school and centre based activities, and it is by following the example of the successful, credible and supportive practitioners that further progress in this joint enterprise will be made.

c) The Schools Council for Curriculum and Examinations

Although the main characteristic of the teachers' centre movement in England and Wales is variation, some common denominators are provided by the Schools Council. For example, every centre receives free copies of the Council's newsletter *Dialogue*, the bi-monthly editions of *Project News*, its Working Papers, and Examination Bulletins, and the annually revised Project Profiles. In addition each centre leader should have access to one of the thirteen field officers, and to the Council's Informa-ation Services. What use is made of these facilities will vary from centre to centre, but their existence is reassuring in a situation where few regular patterns exist.

Information leaflets and posters displayed at teachers' centres play a part in bringing the work of the Schools Council to the attention of teachers, but the Council is now so well established that it has built up a vast collection of literature connected with its various projects. So that some kind of order can be seen in the pro-fusion of activities, the Project Profile Folder has been produced. Each sheet in the folder is a precious source of reference, and an invaluable link between the teachers' centres and 160, Great Portland Street.

The team of field officers form a more personal link between the Council and the centres. Field officers act as Schools Council 'agents', and as they travel from centre to centre, they not only humanize the Council, but also help to link advisers, inspectors, centre leaders, administrators, project directors, and teachers. Schools Council, regional and national Conferences for Teacher's Centre Leaders have in the past also shown the participants that they share a common purpose.

In addition to financing major projects, the Schools Council also uses its resources to support and encourage local curriculum development work. Through the Morrell Funds, awards in the region of £60 to £300 are allocated to study groups, who need help to make a success of work already well in hand. As they visit centres and schools the field officers look for possible award contenders, who might convince the award committee that their materials have a distinctive quality. Present funds have been inadequate to meet the needs of this scheme, and so further money has been allocated by the Council to support local work that has wider implications.

The Schools Council Project Profile Folder contains descriptions of local projects already receiving Council help and finance. Among these is the Swindon Record of Personal Achievement Scheme, which was devised by local teachers working from the Swindon Curriculum Study and Development Centre. It has been in operation since 1970, but an independent evaluator based at the Centre has the opportunity to 'assess the effects which the Record of Personal Achievement may have upon the curriculum and organization of schools and upon teaching methods' and 'make sufficient information available to enable an interested school in another LEA to make an informed decision about the scheme's applicability to its own circumstances'. This Schools Council involvement in a scheme initiated and operated at a local level is an interesting alternative to the normal local implementation of centrally devised schemes.

This Swindon example provides an appropriate bridge between a consideration of the Schools Council's local and national projects, for it is a specific example to support a former Joint Secretary's claim that — 'The Council stands for devolution, and the acceptance of local responsibility' (Light in Watkins (ed), 1973). It is because of the importance placed on devolution, and the need for teachers to find their own solutions to their curriculum problems that the Schools Council has encouraged the work of teachers' centres. Furthermore the work of the Schools Council has been further de-centralized through the setting up of Regional Information Centres, and where these are sited in the same premises as teachers' centres, such as Pendower Hall, Newcastle-upon-Tyne, they can 'bring home' to the classroom teacher that the Council has something to offer *him*.

Cooperation often becomes most productive when a centre is involved in the work of a Council project. This may mean local teachers meeting at a centre to work with a project group such as the 'Education for a Multi-Racial Society' team. For this project, work was begun in two pilot areas and teachers acted as 'guinea pigs' as various approaches to multi-racial education were tried out. The degree of success of these approaches was then evaluated, and the results reported at a national conference for advisers and centre leaders. From this conference came ideas for the setting up of new groups, some of which then met at teachers' centres.

A rather different type of liaison between a Schools Council project team, and teachers' centres was initated by the Director of 'The Curricular Needs of Slow Learning Pupils' Project. A searching questionnaire was sent to all teachers' centres, and some leaders arranged meetings at which the questionnaire was used as a discussion document. The reactions of the teachers were reported to the project team, who have themselves addressed meetings of more than one hundred teacher groups.

The Director of the 'Progress in Learning Science' project has also recognized the need to initiate teachers into the spirit and content of the project. Having met with teachers in centres in six LEAs, the Project Director has modified the original material and, with the help of a teachers' centre leader and a LEA adviser, has devised plans for a network of in-service courses on themes such as 'Making Decisions about the Learning Environment'; these are centrally, locally and school-based. A teachers' centre was used for pilot workshops at which the format of the courses was tried out. The Director of this project, Dr Wynne Harlen, was the evaluator of the 'Science 5—13' project and so her current work is no doubt being influenced by the experience of the 5—13 team, who —

'sought direct contact with a large number of teachers in schools and teachers' centres in order to help them understand project thinking, to stimulate continuing local groups of teachers, and so to work towards teacher self-sufficiency. In this way, teachers directly helped form an important part of the project's output'. (Schools Council, 1973)

Although holding no brief for in-service training, the Council is making increasingly strenuous efforts to facilitate the dissemination of its work. For example, the 'Art and Craft 8—13' project team have produced filmstrips and cassettes in addition to the project's books (Schools Council, 1974) that can be used as discussion material by those involved in teacher education. The filmstrips were shown in trial form at teachers' centres, and then revised according to teachers' reactions.

A closer look at two mathematics projects, shows how the Schools Council's plans are changed, and how groups of teachers, many based at teachers' centres, have influenced curriculum development. The 'Mathematics for the Majority' project team produced guides, which were intended as 'starters' for the production of materials by teachers, working individually or in groups. However

'in this instance, teachers even in groups, are often not in a position to prepare all their own classroom materials for pupil use, and in response to this situation the Council has established a continuation project to develop classroom materials'. (*ibid.*)

The materials have been produced by teachers' writing groups, coordinated by a teachers' centre leader, teacher, or adviser. By recognizing that teachers are often too pressurized to turn good intentions into actions, by providing finance to make teacher release possible, and by involving teachers' centres in this 'Mathematics for the Majority Continuation Project', it has been possible for very flexible and individual materials to be produced.

Although the publishers of the above project have begun to produce materials for pupil use, like those produced by the 'Geography for the Young School Leaver' team, they are devised so as to make individual adaptation easy. This is in keeping with the Schools Council's policy of being non-prescriptive, and of doing all that it can to ensure that its materials are not taken up indiscriminately, without concern for local circumstances. For as Joslyn Owen reminded us in 1973 'official blessing, in terms of the School Council's projects, means no more than that successive trials of sample materials have been carried out'.

Besides inviting teachers to add to, and modify published materials:

'the Council intended its publications to be rapidly plagiarized by other publishers, and its ideas taken up by others who felt they were so good they would produce their own versions'. (Mothersole in Bell and Prescott (eds), 1975)

Just as some teachers' centres produced their own guides to the Nuffield Guides, so some have produced their own materials, using Schools Council work as a model. For instance, some centres have produced further units for teachers on additional 'Science 5—13' topics, and others have taken key concepts suggested in the 'History, Geography, Social Science 8—13 Project' publications, and devised materials tailored to meet the needs of their own pupils.

It is by studying a project's material, considering whether it has a contribution to make to the situation in each school, and then taking appropriate action, which may be sending it back to the publisher, or, alternatively, starting to devise accompanying materials, that leaders prevent the centres from becoming:

'mere outposts for the dissemination of Schools Council orthodoxy, an orthodoxy all the more dangerous and insidious for being unrecognized by the recipients and unsought by the Schools Council itself'. (Richards, 1972)

Despite this caution against orthodoxy, it seems that much of the criticism at present being levelled at the Schools Council is aimed at its limited effectiveness especially in the field of dissemination. Evidence suggests that far from encouraging orthodoxy, the proliferation of project material may have failed to 'bridge the credibility gap' for many teachers not involved in the development stages of project work. However, few large projects are now being initiated and one team has been brought together with the sole purpose of investigating the take-up of project material. (Impact and Take-up of Schools Council Projects) In addition, the Chairman of the Schools Council, Sir Alex Smith, is himself currently making informal fact-finding visits to teachers' centres, and other educational establishments in order to talk with and listen to teachers. It is to be hoped that the 'Impact' project and the concerted effort of Schools Council staff and members of its committees to re-think its contribution to the educational system, without losing the best from more affluent days, will be accompanied by cooperation from the centres who can become even more influential agencies for curriculum improvement.

d) Other educational bodies

Besides being host to several Schools Council projects, the National Foundation for Educational Research is the most important independent body engaged in educational research in this country. It publishes its own journal and acts as a 'clearing house' for research information. In order to make more teachers aware of the NFER, its publishing company in collaboration with its Information Division is establishing regional displays of publications and research information, and of the six venues so far selected two of these are in teachers' centres. Teachers' centre leaders sometimes seek help from the NFER, when they have problems connected with research and assessment and the Foundation sometimes uses teachers' centre facilities when a project director needs to work with teachers. For example the director of a project on assessment techniques in science teaching, met with small groups of teachers in several LEA centres, and her materials are being adapted in the light of the work done by teachers with their pupils. Similarly a current Schools Council project team, based at the NFER and entitled 'Record keeping in the Primary School', is considering different aspects of record-keeping with the help of study groups based at teachers' centres in various parts of the country.

Some teachers' centres also have links with a more recently created educational body — the Open University, which sometimes uses centre premises for its activities. University staff are investigating the feasibility of using teachers' centres as study centres, and some centres have been particularly involved in the 'Reading Development' course. Centres in two counties were used when the course material was being devised and tested. With the help of centre leaders and LEAs, tutorial sessions connected with the course are held at some centres. Tutorial staff from the Open University's Institute of Educational Technology also work with groups of teachers in local centres. These links should be fruitful especially as half of the first wave of Open University graduates were teachers.

Every teachers' centre receives from the BBC, regular

information on all aspects of schools and FE output, but centres sometimes become more involved with the BBC's work through its in-service training series. Study groups have met in teachers' centres to discuss radio series such as 'Teaching Young Readers' and TV series on 'Raising of the School Leaving Age', 'Early Years at School', and the more recent 'Middle Years at School'. A BBC Education Officer reports that the teachers' centres have played a very important role in the utilization of these series.

In addition, at meetings held at teachers' centres and other places, BBC Education Officers are able to obtain 'feedback', which can be considered during the planning stages of future broadcasts. Furthermore many teachers' centres are helping the schools by mass-producing material for BBC broadcasts so that unnecessary repetition of the same task in many separate establishments can be avoided.

Where local radio stations exist some teachers have become involved in the actual production of programmes, and some independent radio and TV companies now work closely with teachers. Several local radio stations broadcast series that need to be used in conjunction with resource materials produced at local teachers' centres. ATV has also held conferences for teachers' centre leaders at which improved liaison has been discussed.

Another gathering for teachers' centre leaders was organized by the Department of Management and Business Studies at Brighton Polytechnic. The purpose of the conference was for the leaders to learn management techniques that would help them work more efficiently. In a different type of attempt to capitalize on specialist expertise, some centres cooperate with colleges of technology, and further education colleges in the running of AVA and reprographic courses. Furthermore as a result of initiatives taken by the Institute of Physics, the Chemical Society and the Institute of Biology, teachers' centres of a different nature than those set up by the LEAs have been established with bases in universities, colleges, polytechnics and schools. These centres provide specialist help particularly for secondary colleagues often under-serviced by LEA centres. However, as I.F. Roberts (1975) reports, these centres which often specialize in only one of the sciences may have to make changes in their approach in order to adapt to the swing towards integration.

Centre meetings of a more independent nature are arranged by subject associations — 'Associations of teachers of English, mathematics, history, geography, art and remedial work are all regular visitors to certain centres, and as a result, many become committed to curriculum development'. (Braithwaite, 1971)

Although teachers' unions often use the centres for their meetings, links with these bodies are not always as close as might be expected. However, the NUT carried out 'A survey of the conditions of service of Teachers' Centre Leaders and conditions of teacher participation in Centre activities' in 1971 (NUT, 1972) and in the Autumn of 1974 it distributed a questionnaire on the salaries and conditions of service of the professional staff of teachers' centres. This Union has also set up an Advisory Committee to concern itself with the work of teachers' centres.

As the number of teachers' centres has grown so groups of leaders have met together to discuss subjects of common concern. The Icknield Wardens, and the Wardens in the South East (WISE) are just two examples of groups of leaders that meet regularly. Through WISE the first national course/conference was held at the London Institute in 1971. From this beginning has evolved the National Conference of Teachers' Centre Leaders, which was established in 1973. This body is not a union, is non-political, and claims to be more like a teaching-subject association. Membership is £2.50 per annum, and it had its own newsletter *Centre* now replaced by a journal *Insight*. Now that teachers' centres have lost some of their novelty appeal this association which is open to other colleagues besides centre leaders, may enable all concerned with their progress to meet new challenges with fewer doubts caused by the insecurity of isolation. It has certainly given teachers' centre leaders a national 'voice', which has been listened to during the post-James discussions on the future of in-service education.

Chapter 6

The James Report and the White Paper's Implications for Teachers' Centres

a) General

It is interesting to note that in Appendix 2 of the James Report we read that while the Association of Teachers of Spanish and Portuguese, the North Surrey Dyslexic Society, and the Society of Industrial Tutors submitted written evidence for the consideration of the James Committee, the Wardens in the South East appear to be the only teachers' centre group to have done so. Also, although the Committee visited twenty-three colleges of education, and thirteen schools or institutes of education, teachers' centres in only two LEAs appear on the 'visited list'.

These observations having been made, it seems that teachers' centres did not escape the notice of Lord James and his committee of six. In fact, a member of the committee, Mr C. P. Milroy reported at a Study Conference held at Clacton in 1972 that 'The development of teachers' centres played an important part in the committee's thinking'. This influence can be detected in many of the Report's recommendations, but more important for the future, is the 'pride of place' that James gives to Third Cycle activities, for it is with the professional activities of serving teachers that teachers' centres are already so intimately involved.

b) Towards the establishment of professional centres

The James Report (DES, 1972) claims that through increased Third Cycle provision — 'the quality of our education, and the standards of the profession can be most speedily, powerfully, and economically improved' — and it is suggested the formation of professional centres will enable this improvement to take place. However, there is some confusion over professional centre terminology. If this recommendation of James is acted upon, a college of education may be a professional institution and a professional centre in so far as it will continue its First Cycle activities, whilst also acting as a professional centre for Second Cycle work with inductees, or Third Cycle programmes for serving teachers. Also, some teachers' centres will continue with their present name and form, while others will become professional centres if they satisfy the requirements of the yet to be formed regional bodies. The name professional centre could also be used as a 'blanket' term to describe the area's educational institutions involved in Second and Third Cycle work. So a teachers' centre could be a professional centre, and/or part of a professional centre matrix. In either case it seems that James had not forgotten McNair, for in Chapter Two, we read —

'Professional centres, whether based on professional institutions, or elsewhere, would become a forum for the exchange of ideas, information and experience, between new and experienced teachers, teacher trainers and LEA advisers'.

Obviously such 'forums' would bear close resemblance to the education centres suggested in the 1944 Report.

Variety has been repeatedly singled out as a feature of English educational establishments in general, and of teachers' centres in particular, and it seems that uniformity will also evade professional centres, whether the term describes a conceptual framework, a more easily charted matrix, or a single establishment. A member of the Report committee, Dr Harry Judge, speaking at a Schools Council Regional Study Conference at Canterbury in 1972 prepares us for variety, but also predicts some coherence —

'If professional centres are to provide for anything from twenty-two to eight thousand teachers, few generalizations about their structures can be risked. Coherence for their work will, of course, be provided by the professional committee'.

Existing teachers' centres have variation in their committee structure, membership, and nomenclature, but with relatively minor adjustments, most could conform to the James' recommendation for the professional committee.

Not only is teachers' centre committee structure in line with the James' proposals, but so also is the name given to most teachers' centre leaders. The title 'Warden' has generally been avoided in this study, because so many other names are also used, and because teachers' centre leader is the name adopted by their first national association. However, in the James Report there is no such avoidance, for each professional centre

> 'would have a full-time warden, of at least senior lecturer status, who would be selected by the centres management committee, approved by the regional body, and paid by the LEA. He would have an independent role, and his chief responsibility would be to draw upon available sources to meet the training requirements of the teachers served by his centre' (DES, 1972).

This emphasis on the warden's independent role, and the designation of a professional centre as 'a point of reference independent of school and their employers' is in line with the existing situation in most teachers' centres. The Report goes on to encourage wardens to teach in local schools, and this confirms him as a classroom practitioner, rather than as a 'desk-bound administrator'.

If we turn from personnel to premises, we find that the Report favours accommodation that is not too large, for colleagues should be able to 'develop a sense of personal engagement in the work'. (*ibid.*) To be in keeping with the Report's suggestions, professional centres should have a workshop, tutorial room, common room, and resource facilities. This type of set-up is similar to that in most teachers' centres so that the James suggestion that professional centres, other than those housed in existing professional institutions should be 'in many cases developed from existing teachers' centres' (*ibid.*), should not be difficult to arrange. The recommendation that use should be made of the specialized facilities, such as gymnasia and laboratories in other establishments is also confirmation of present teachers' centre practice.

James gave so much support to the expansion of Third Cycle activities which require school release and secondment, that one might have expected the part-time and short-term activities that make up such a large part of teachers' centre programmes would be given less emphasis. However, such a trend would be at variance with the Report's recommendation that 'The development of longer and full-time courses should not be bought at the expense of those valuable short-term activities, which should themselves be expanded considerably'. (*ibid.*) In addition, the Report commends another mainstay of teachers' centre activities, curriculum development, as a worthy activity for the Third Cycle. Also, we have seen how closely the Schools Council has worked with evolving teachers' centres, and so it is heartening to read that participation in Council development is also seen as a worthwhile Third Cycle activity.

Existing links between teachers' centres and the LEA advisory services have been described in Chapter 5, where it was also suggested that in many cases these links could be improved. James would seem to be in favour of such improvement for he apportions an important place to advisers in a new system, on the grounds that

'They are in close touch with schools, will be aware of their day-to-day problems and able to assess needs as they arise and to make or suggest immediate arrangements to meet them'.

Immediacy has been a feature of teachers' centre activity, and with increased help from travelling advisers, it may be possible to prevent the development of an impersonal and bureaucratic organization in the professional centres.

The James Report having been compiled, published and scrutinized, the government then responded with the White Paper *Education: A Framework for Expansion* (DES, 1972). As far as Third Cycle proposals were concerned, at that time the government foresaw that 1981 would be the year by which time three per cent of the teaching population would be absent from the schools on secondment at one time. In the meantime, it proposed that during the 1974-5 academic year, pilot schemes should be organized so that ways and means could be found for the successful introduction of the professional tutor. However, in these schemes the tutors were to concern themselves only with newly qualified teachers, thus avoiding the other two parts of

James' proposed triple responsibility for students on teaching practice, and teachers' in-service education coordination.

c) Towards a new induction year

Because of the deteriorating financial situation only Liverpool and Northumberland survived to become pilot areas for the induction of new teachers, but reports of these schemes do provide us with illustrative evidence of James on trial. However, it should be remembered that the present 'newly qualified teachers', as the probationers are called in the reports, have undergone traditional college courses, rather than the 'Jamesian alternatives'.

The organization of the Liverpool Scheme brought together administrators, advisers, colleges of education, schools, the university, and the Liverpool Teachers' Centre. A new Administrative Section for Teacher Development was set up, an adviser was made responsible for the Scheme, and a research fellow attached to Liverpool University School of Education was given the task of evaluation. An advisory committee of forty-six members was called together in 1973, and included in the total are many teachers (teachers' representatives on Education Committee — three; one representative from each Teachers' Association — seven; representative teachers from each stage of education — seven; representatives of probationary teachers — two, and headteachers of non-maintained schools — two. In addition, Liverpool Teachers' Centre has one place, and there are also places for the eight coordinators at the professional centres). Allocation of so many committee places to teachers is in line with James' suggestion, that the schools should have a greater part in the preparation its prospective members.

The James Report recommended that each school should have a professional tutor, and in Liverpool with two exceptions this advice was followed. Of course it should be remembered that in this Scheme, only schools with newly qualified teachers would have teacher tutors (as they have been 'labelled' in Liverpool) because of the restricted introduction of the professional tutor concept. Teacher tutors were appointed by Managing Bodies from existing members of staff. In the event, nearly half of the Liverpool appointments went to heads or deputy heads, but in Northumberland, where they were actively discouraged from applying for the posts, the proportion was far less.

The schools were attached to one of the professional centres on a mainly geographical basis, and it is reassuring to read that

'The existing teachers' centre was an obvious choice for one professional centre (junior schools)'. (Liverpool Education Committee, 1975)

It may be significant, that attached to this teachers' centre, are an EPA Centre, and a Priority Centre of which the teachers' centre principal is also the director. The remaining professional centres were located in colleges of education, two of which had specialist responsibility for home economics and women's PE. Each centre appointed coordinators, and working parties were set up to formulate induction programmes for that centre. Each working party consisted of one head teacher, two teacher tutors, three advisers, four newly qualified teachers, and five professional centre staff members.

As these programmes were being devised, working party members were mindful of R. Bolam's Bristol research which concluded in 1973

'that the overwhelming concern of most probationers is with the practicalities of their own teaching situation and that practical reliance is the principal yardstick by which they will judge any induction programme. It is therefore recommended that the broad aim of the programme should be to offer practical and individual help to probationers, and that the main focus should be upon the problems and opportunities facing them in their own schools and classrooms'.

The induction programme took place partly in the schools, partly in the professional centre, and partly in other establishments, but all the time, emphasis was given to the practical and the relevant, and this emphasis is in line with the importance given by teachers' centres to everyday classroom problems and opportunities. To illustrate the practicality of the proposed plans, Report 5 on the Induction Programme contains a list of possible group topics which include 'Registration Procedures', 'Planning Lessons', and 'How to read a Story'. In Appendix I of Report 5, there is also the suggestion that a 'Directory of Skills' should be drawn up by each professional centre —

> 'This would list schools which have acquired particular
> expertise and experience in a certain field, which a newly
> qualified teacher seeking help in that particular field, could
> visit by arrangement . . .' (Liverpool Education Committee,
> 1975)

The Liverpool Scheme has been criticized for containing too
many gimmicks, so it is to be hoped that this Directory idea will
not present so many organizational problems that it remains at
the gimmick stage.

In order to prepare the teacher tutors for their task, ten one-day
briefing sessions were arranged for the summer term of 1974. The
guidelines for the briefing sessions were prepared by a Sub-
Committee set up by the scheme's Advisory Committee. To
allocate only ten days for the preparation of teacher tutors for their
task, is to allow far less time than was suggested in the James
Report, but in view of the magnitude of national implementation
of the scheme, it may be a realistic alternative. The teacher tutors
attached to professional centres located in colleges of education
were able to visit the teachers' centre during one of their briefing
sessions, in order to find out about the services it might offer the
newly qualified teachers and themselves.

The sixty-nine teacher tutors attached to the Professional
Centre at the Liverpool Teachers' Centre were divided into two
groups, and included in their briefing days were visits to a local
college, and time spent on such themes as 'Com-
munication/Counselling/Stress' and 'New Thinking and
Practice'. The latter was introduced by the then Principal of the
teachers' centre, Dr Eric Midwinter. The morning of briefing day
was spent on an exploration of the Teachers' Centres' part in the
Induction Scheme, and the deputy head of a comprehensive
school and Dr Midwinter gave a talk entitled 'The Teachers'
Centre as a Professional Centre'. The teacher tutors had the opportunity to examine the Centre's resources, its curriculum development facilities, and to visit the Home-School Unit.

Part of the Liverpool teacher-tutor's task has been to help
newly qualified teachers gain support from the professional
centre to which they are attached. Because of this, it has been

important for him to bear in mind the 'local courses and resources to which individual probationers need to be referred. Teacher tutors should become especially familiar with the projected work of local professional centres'. (*ibid.*) Many existing teachers' centres have teacher representatives or correspondents in the schools which they serve, and it would seem that teachers who have acted in this capacity would be well prepared for this part of the teacher tutor role.

It is suggested in the Pilot Scheme's Fifth Report that teacher tutors should meet regularly at a professional centre on a rota basis during the year. Through such meetings, colleagues should be able to exchange ideas, and provide each other with much needed support. In addition, it is suggested that

'At intervals during the year, but especially in the probationers' first term, social functions should be arranged in the evening at which teacher tutors, professional centre staff, and probationers could meet informally'. (Hill, 1975)

The need for this type of socialization was shown by the result of Dale and Taylor's influential 'Survey of Teachers in the First Year of Service' (1971), and as was pointed out in Chapter 4 Section (e) of this study, some teachers' centres already provide colleagues with a programme of social activities which would satisfy this requirement.

The Pilot Scheme's Reports show that guidelines for the teacher tutor briefing sessions, and the programmes for the newly qualified teacher's one day per week spent on induction activities have been carefully planned, and in many cases committed to paper, but both frame-works left plenty of room for necessary adjustment. Time was allowed for discussion, plenary sessions, teacher tutor options, and for activities suggested by the newly qualified teachers. Such flexibility would seem imperative, especially in a pilot scheme that has resulted from the James Report, which placed so much emphasis on the need to cater for the *varying* problems of young teachers.

Although Liverpool has educational problems connected with urbanization, it is a relatively compact LEA, and access to professional centres cannot have caused as many problems as in the other Pilot area. Lord James stressed the need for professional

centres to be within easy reach of a large number of schools, and in
our major cities this is generally easy, but there may be obstacles
ahead in areas where there are great distances between schools,
and in the DES Report on Education No. 84, 1976, Baker and
Bolam summarize many of the induction schemes being used in
other authorities.

The ease with which the Liverpool Teachers' Centre has been
drawn into the Pilot Scheme also highlights the difference
between it, and many centres in small towns. The Liverpool
Centre has extensive premises, generous financial backing, and an
experienced support staff. A very different situation exists in
authorities that have many scattered centres, which are far less
developed. However, *necessity* demands that new entrants to the
profession should take part in induction programmes based in
centres not far from their schools, so *invention* is required to help
small centres play a constructive part in their LEAs response to the
Liverpool and Northumberland Pilot Schemes.

d) Towards progression in in-service education and training

Besides criticizing the existing arrangements for the induction
of new entrants to the teaching profession, the James Report,
despite advocating a mammoth increase in in-service education,
criticized the existing provision on several counts. One of these
was 'that existing courses are not clearly related to defined stages
in an individual's career, or to the initial training that preceded it'.
This judgment should come as no surprise, for this examination
of teachers' centres has shown that although many colleagues
approach in-service activities with interest, there seems to be no
underlying rationale or development connected with this
participation.

In an effort to stimulate consideration that may lead to an
improvement of this situation, a sub-committee of the DES
'Advisory Committee on the Supply and Training of Teachers'
(ACSTT) prepared the first of a series of discussion papers on in-
service education and training (INSET). This document was sent
out to LEAs, colleges and departments of education, ATOs, and
other interested bodies in November 1974, with the request that
responses should be submitted by the end of that year.

The paper, which is introduced by H. A. Harding, summarizes
the value of INSET, both to individual teachers and to their

employers, and then in the following words supports the criticism
made previously by James —

'It is difficult to discern in this progression any relationships of
the parts to the whole, or of any unifying principle other than
the fact that serving teachers are participants'. (DES, 1974)

It then goes on to describe a career profile that might provide a
framework for INSET progression.

The first stage in the development would be induction, which if
the James Report is implemented would be a Second Cycle
activity. In the four to six years after induction, it is suggested that
teachers need 'a series of relatively short courses which are specific
in their content and application'. DES/ATO courses are quoted
as being suitable for this stage, and it is probable that many
existing teachers' centres already arrange courses that are
appropriate for this early career period, but unfortunately they are
advertised generally, and applied for indiscriminately.

The discussion paper suggests that after five to eight years of
teaching, many colleagues are ready for a period of orientation.
This is a time when many teachers are making decisions about
their careers, and it is suggested that secondment for a term could
provide the necessary study opportunities. Such study seems likely
to be based at a college of education, but if some teachers' centres
develop areas of excellence, particularly in curriculum development, such orientation periods could usefully be spent in the production and evaluation of classroom materials. Through such
activity, teachers could acquire experience linked with practice,
from which they might gain insight that later would save them
from some of the superficialities of schooling. The work of the
teachers' centres would also be enriched through involvement in
such study, especially if it had classroom application.

In the period after this secondment, the sub-committee suggest
that

'there would seem to be the need for further studies on a part-
time/full-time basis, somewhat similar in length to the specific
courses outlined above, but, different in character and higher in
standard'. (*ibid.*)

These activities are labelled 'advanced seminars', and it is proposed that they should be a preparation for advanced study courses, which should be undertaken after twelve to fifteen years in the profession. Although few teachers' centres seem equipped or staffed for these 'advanced' activities, those who do advanced work in other establishments should be encouraged to share their experiences by becoming tutors for 'specific' INSET activities and group leaders for curriculum development. If school responsibilities can be combined with the challenges of teachers' centre group leadership, it may be possible for the schools to gain more benefit from these staff with advanced qualifications. This would seem highly desirable, for at present many courses merely qualify their participants for a departure from the 'coal-face'.

The writers of the discussion paper suggest that after colleagues have reached the mid-point in their career, they may need preparation for top management posts, or alternatively, for refreshment. Universities and polytechnics seem best suited to provide courses to meet the first need, and a wide variety of educational and non-educational establishments (and even travel companies) could provide the 'break' needed by so many teachers in the second half of their teaching lives. A further discussion paper was distributed from the DES in August 1975, and included in the paper was a tabulated framework which suggested patterns for INSET under the headings

1. Resources, Facilities and Services.
2. Management and Consultative Arrangements, and
3. INSET work undertaken.

Under the first heading it is suggested that local teachers' centres should have accommodation for lectures and discussions, a workshop and audiovisual facilities, display areas and social facilities. The management and consultative column for teachers' centres consists of warden / wardens and teachers' committee. In column three the following INSET work was suggested —

'Short courses of immediate professional relevance. Longer courses were justified by local demand e.g. on day release basis. Informal working groups. Demonstration of materials. Close liaison with colleges and departments of education and schools'.

Following consideration arising from the two discussion papers, the Induction and In-Service Sub-Committee of the ACSTT presented a report with recommendations to the Secretary of State for urgent consideration in August 1976. Over-riding themes of the Report are the need for coordination, the avoidance of duplication, and the improved use of existing institutions. The Report gives special emphasis to school-focussed INSET activities, and in Section 3 paragraph 6, the following functions for teachers' centres are suggested —

'With a full-time professional warden and steering committee representing teachers, the LEA and major institutions including universities, and given a reasonable measure of autonomy, these can serve as a valuable catalyst for the immediate needs of teachers and schools in a locality. Their best role is to concentrate on the immediate relevant needs of teachers and school-focussed activities. They should also serve as centres of information and be able to refer to the appropriate source teachers who wish to pursue their studies in greater depth. They can also be centres through which major institutions and universities make their resources more widely available. The availability of centres, however modest, in rural areas is of vital importance'.

In view of the dangers to rural centres caused by financial cut-backs, the final sentence would seem to be particularly significant. The recommendation for Steering Committee membership shows an enlargement of the suggestion contained in Discussion Paper 2, but this would seem desirable provided the Committee do not become too remote so that they can act only in a 'rubber stamping' capacity. In general the Report seems to have been greeted with approval by those committed to the retention of local bases for the growth of the teachers' responsibility for professional development through the different phases outlined in the ACSTT Discussion Paper of 1974 (DES).

e) Towards a coordinated in-service education and training programme

The lack of progression in Third Cycle activities was not the only fault found by the James Committee in existing INSET arrangements —

'facilities, inadequate in themselves are not always well coordinated, so that even within a limited programme there may still be some wasteful duplication of effort'. (DES, 1972)

The haphazard nature of teachers' centre provision has been a recurring feature of this study, and it seems that the James Committee were also struck by the apparent lack of pattern, cohesion, or decipherable rationale in the 'in-service jungle'.

In order to provide coordination, the Report suggests that at a national level, an agency with perhaps the name 'National Council for Teacher Education and Training' (NCTET) should be set up; and at the regional level 'Regional Councils for Colleges and Departments of Education' (RCCDE) need to be established. It is suggested that there should perhaps be fifteen regional councils, each with two or three universities, one or two polytechnics, and about ten colleges. Also, they should be free of some of the geographical anomalies that are a feature of the ATOs, which they will replace. Each professional institution within the region would be represented on the RCCDE and there should be

'five teacher representatives from schools and further education, chosen for their professional standing, whose value would be all the greater if they did not regard themselves as mandated representatives of the associations'. (DES, 1972)

This proviso would seem to be directed at one present shortcoming of union representation on many committees, but it also supports practice in many teachers' centres where 'unattached' professionals contribute to the running of committees. Additionally, the RCCDE would have an academic and a professional committee, as well as any necessary sub-committees.

So far as teachers' centres are concerned, RCCDEs would be important because of their coordinating and designating functions. In connection with the second function the vital words would seem to be —

'Unless a centre satisfied the professional criteria defined by its regional body, it would not be able to function as a professional centre'. (*ibid.*)

Potential professional centres will be eager to discover what these 'professional criteria' will be, and how they can satisfy them. In the meantime there should be no lack of incentives for teachers' centres, to improve their professional services to the schools with which they are connected.

While awaiting guidance regarding the setting up of RCCDEs, some LEAs are attempting to coordinate in-service education, within their own boundaries. It is to be hoped that 'spade-work' performed at LEA level will be helpful to the RCCDEs, but a great advantage of the regional councils is that they will be able to override any shortsighted LEA decisions. However, it is important that LEAs should prepare their briefs, for implicit in the James' Report's proposals, and the ACSTT sub-committee's recommendations is the need for consultative machinery at the local level.

One LEA has a consultative group with membership of thirty, with places allocated to teachers, head teachers and principals, the LEA, colleges of education, and the university, and to HMIs and Schools Council observers. Four of the teacher representatives are nominated by the Teachers' Consultative Committee, but the other teacher places are allocated to representatives of teachers' centre committees and wardens. The total for the latter could be four, five or six, as co-option is allowed to ensure balance of stage, type of school, or other interest. These details are important for they show that at least one LEA recognizes that teachers' centre users can play an important part in reporting teacher opinion.

Proposals for professional centres have been advanced, and details of the regional councils are awaited with interest, but it would be unfortunate if an impression was given that the setting up of centres and organizational machinery will be sufficient conditions for the improvement of INSET arrangements. The North West Regional Project is possibly the most appropriate model on which regional developments could be based, and that Project's Director reminds us that there are many intangibles on which success depends. In our quest for efficiency and coordination, we should note that he attributes much of the success in the North

West to the fact that

> 'the leader's work was emotionally and professionally satis-
> fying, offering him also the experience of personal development
> and some evidence of the impact of his efforts upon the schools'.
> (Rudd in Watkins (ed), 1973)

Chapter 7

Pedagogic Centres within the Norwegian Educational System

'Geographical features and local needs are both factors in determining the type of centre which is set up'. (Braithwaite, 1971)

These words of a former Schools Council field officer refer to teachers' centres in England and Wales, but they provide an apt link with Pedagogic Centres in Norway, for in this country geography has played a special part in the development of all educational establishments. Norway's area is only just larger than the United Kingdom's but she has a 1,650 mile long coastline, and in Europe distances are only greater in the Soviet Union. Great distances between schools and communities, coupled with differences caused by the ruggedness of the terrain and hazards connected with a harsh climate, has meant that planners have had to give special attention to travel and communication considerations.

The first centre was set up in Oslo in 1969. However, a beginning in the capital city, which is so totally different from most of the remaining areas in Norway, could have been misleading. As in other countries advocates of equality for all are persistently confronted with problems that are caused by inequality of population distribution. Bergen, Trondheim and Sandnes set up centres soon after Oslo had done so, but even these cities and towns are quite different from places like Seljord, where a centre was established more recently. In the rural district that the

Seljord Centre serves, there are only thirty-two teachers, and between three and four hundred pupils. Even legislation reflects these differences, for until 1959 there were different laws governing urban and rural schools in Norway.

However the problems of the isolated school in the fjord, on the island, or near the mountain top, and of the colleagues in the remote two-teacher schools are typical of those faced in sparsely populated countries. They are also small scale examples of Scandinavia's general isolation problem. Being positioned in a 'backwater of Europe', the countries appear to need to prove themselves. Fortunately, Norway has a long Atlantic facing coastline, and her tradition for exploration, discovery, and peace-making may have made her more outward-looking and flexible in bids to find solutions to her problems.

In 1954 the Act on Experiment and Innovation in Education was passed by the National Assembly, and as a result the National Council for Innovation in Education was set up in the same year. A major outcome of these combined events, has been the introduction of the Monster Plan in 1967. This Model Plan gives

'A detailed account of the aims set for the school, and its educational purposes, and of the allocation of subjects and lessons, and of the teaching programmes for all subjects and at all class-levels, for ordinary auxiliary and special teaching'. (Horge in Interskola, 1973)

Adoption of the plan has resulted in the setting up of Pedagogic Centres, and the appointment of advisers and part-time advisory teachers to facilitate the necessary changes.

This pattern of change is interesting when parallels are drawn between the English and Norwegian systems. The influence of the Lutheran Church, the long struggle to regain and then retain independence, and a desire to give equal opportunities through legislative edicts, has resulted in Norway's strongly centralized educational system. A comparison between the Schools Council for England and Wales and Norway's National Council for Innovation in Education shows up differences between centralized and decentralized systems. The products of projects sponsored by the Schools Council survive and are extended, or 'shiver and die' according to the response they receive from classroom practitioners; whereas the materials recommended by the National Council for Innovation in Education, must allegedly be accepted by teachers, even if they are considered unsuitable for their purposes. The difficulties surrounding the latter would seem to be those connected with attitudinal change. It seems likely that colleagues who are unconvinced of the Monster Plan's merit will either struggle to adopt it wholeheartedly regardless of their doubts, or adopt it superficially, and beneath the facade continue to work in the same way as they have always done.

The establishment of Pedagogic Centres is an acknowledgement by administration that even such a carefully prepared model as the Monster Plan needs local premises and personnel to ease its adoption. Although the Plan has clearly defined objectives and guidelines, it does give teachers some room for flexibility, which means that they need to be exposed to a wider selection of materials than they have been in the past. Centres are building up libraries of books and teaching aids so that teachers can become better informed on what is available. This need is most acutely felt in small schools that are isolated by mountains, rivers, ice and lakes.

'The lack of awareness of the kind of material available and the lack of information on how the various textbooks and teaching materials can best be used in schools having few divisions have meant that teachers have not been pressing enough in their demands'. (Hansen in Interskola, 1973)

Linking the new materials to the needs of schools is often the task of the Pedagogic Advisers, who are frequently based at the centres. At one large centre there are eighteen individual advisers with the following separate areas of interest — Special Education, Mathematics, Primary Education, Domestic Science, German, Audiovisual Aids, Machine and Tool Care, English, Counselling, Gymnastics, Music (two advisers), Art (three inspectors), Textiles (two advisers), and Environmental Studies. A large proportion of the work of the advisers is connected with teachers' courses, but they also visit schools regularly to make contacts and recommendations. These visits are particularly welcomed by teachers in small schools, who often have to depend upon complicated road-boat-train communication networks, if they want to attend area meetings.

One way in which teachers in isolated communities can be made to feel 'less' 'cut off', is through the receipt of centre news-letters. One centre's publication is called simply *Kontakt Og Informasgon*. Teachers submit articles and commentaries for the newsletter, which is circulated four times a year to all the local schools. This type of communication may encourage teachers to link up with colleagues who are not too far away and to seek help from advisers, for their customary two visits a year may only rarely be timed to meet the most serious needs.

Norwegians have been compelled to use their ingenuity to solve the schooling problems of localities where there are only a few children in each group. In some cases children are moved from one district to another so that economic class units can be arranged. This ingenuity, which has been developed by national efforts to overcome the restrictions of the terrain, is also brought to play in order to make flexible use of Pedagogic Centres and advisers. For example, communities with large populations can support separate centres, but sparsely populated districts often combine to make a shared centre a viable proposition. Similarly, in the cities full-time advisers are employed, but in less populated areas, advisers are only employed for a certain proportion of each week. For instance, in Drammen which has a population of fifty thousand there are thirteen advisers who are involved with centre work for between eight and ten lessons each week (each lesson being equal to a ninety minute period). In the very rural areas, centres have fewer hours at their disposal for the employment of advisers. Because of this, it is necessary to concentrate on three or four subjects at one time. After a period of about three years, the subjects may be changed, so that most of the subjects will be covered in about ten years.

One of the tasks of the advisers and the other centre staff is to encourage teachers to use their own initiative, for, due to the effects of centralization, many of them have become — in the words of a centre leader — 'slaves to the textbooks'. The Monster Plan encourages them to break away from this 'slavery', but as one leader commented in correspondence — 'This is for the Norwegian teacher a new and unknown world, and it is met with some reluctance'. Many of the centres produce teaching resources for the schools, and some engage teachers to devise materials that have local content. At one centre, sixty booklets have been produced, and six hundred of each have been printed. Other centres report that they have made collections of resources that are connected with the history, literature, songs, music, geology, plants, animals, and so on, of their own district.

In addition to the hazardous nature of the landscape and the resulting communication problems, the Norwegian terrain has also yielded poor crops and so the people have been hard-pressed to survive. In fact only 3.2 per cent of the land is suitable for farming, and only one-third of that is tillable. The increased use of hydro-electric power, and the promise of riches from North Sea oil, have given the country brighter prospects, but traditionally its people have had to take full advantage of every available resource. Consequently, cooperative ventures have been encouraged, and this cooperation is exemplified by the Pedagogic Centre's coordinating role in the field of educational technology. At most centres a wide range of audiovisual and reprographic equipment is available for use and reference, and in one particular centre a group of teachers have collected data and information regarding overhead projectors, typewriters, cine-projectors, and filmstrips — and then sent the details to schools so that colleagues might act on recommendations from fellow-teachers. In another centre recordings of four hundred radio programmes are made each year, and over one thousand copies are sent out to the schools. At a further centre a supply of educational films, video-cassette programmes, and sound recordings of school broadcasts is available. Through this sharing based on the centres, the schools are being helped to overcome the shortages that persistently plague small units.

Before Pedagogic Centres were set up in Norway, some reference was made to the Audiovisual Centres in Sweden and Denmark. This fact is mentioned because it reminds us not only of the cooperation that exists between the Scandinavian countries, because of their close geographical proximity, but also that Norway is less prosperous than Sweden, and is constantly trying to keep pace with the advances in educational technology that are made in that country with alarming rapidity. Bearing this Swedish influence in mind, it is interesting to note that Norway, with its coastline facing the British Isles, and with its historical links with the United Kingdom has also felt the influence of Britain on its Pedagogic Centres. Tutors from this country have conducted workshop sessions in the Norwegian centres, and many British and American publications and products are made available for teacher inspection.

In communities where it is possible to employ a centre leader with good ancillary help, and 'a strong army' of advisers, it seems that the advisers deal more with the teachers, while the centre leader coordinates the whole programme and has fairly wide duties which include the provision of information and orientation to parents and members of local school boards. Parents and local communities have traditionally taken an active interest in the schools:

> 'the schools are in a very special sense the people's schools, and ·
> they are required to give conscious expression of the people's
> needs and aspirations'. (Mallinson, 1974)

Where centres aim to serve a wider interest, these 'needs and aspirations' should be given even greater expression.

However it seems that strong communal feeling and participation can sometimes hinder the extension of centre involvement. In the words of one centre leader:

> 'Teachers may come to the centre any time after school, in the
> evening and the afternoons, however it rarely happens. I don't
> think that this indicates that there is no use for a Pedagogic
> Centre. However, the teachers are engaged in all kinds of social,
> and political or religious work — they've got their families, etc.
> . . . I think it is right to get in touch with teachers at day-time'.

Teachers' centre leaders in England often reflect on the alternative activities that prevent centre participation, so it is interesting to read this Norwegian leader's suggestion that 'political', 'religious', 'social', and 'family' commitments stand in the way of centre involvement.

Community interest in the work of Pedagogic Centres is illustrated in a totally different way by an example of local intervention. In a town with about thirty-four thousand inhabitants, a centre was set up in 1970, but in 1973 a group under the town council was appointed to estimate its value, and to find ways of decreasing its expenditure. However, after a year of investigations, the group has recommended that the centre should be given more recognition, and that higher expenditure is necessary if the work is to be properly accomplished. This participation on behalf of the people had encouraging results, and in the December of 1974, the centre leader was able to write — 'Because of this inquiry we are looking forward to better times in the future'. It will be interesting to see whether increasing concern being paid by county councillors and other elected members in English teachers' centres will result in expansion.

The cooperative spirit seen in so much of Norway's national way of life is also illustrated in the provision of teachers' in-service education. Courses are planned by the advisers in partnership with the teacher training schools and the universities. Despite this cooperation, a teachers' centre leader reports —

> 'Teachers in the elementary schools feel that 'specialists' do not *know* the problems, and very little about how to solve the problems in the elementary schools. Therefore one of our main tasks now will be to find out how to *get together and teach each other*'.

This same problem has by no means been solved in England and Wales, but it would seem that this is one area in which colleagues from England and Norway could gain much from a greater sharing of experiences. Fruitful though such sharing might be, it would be dangerous to transfer successful ideas and methods from one country to another without taking into account the unique characteristics of the nations concerned. In the case of Norway any innovators would do well to remember that —

> 'If ever geography has influenced national history, and moulded national character it must be in Norway'. (Dixon, 1965)

Chapter 8

Teachers' Centres in the USA

a) In context

Just as 'insular security' has made it possible for variety and individuality to flourish in England and Wales, and as the ruggedness of the terrain has been highly influential in the development of the Norwegian educational system, so also have geographical features had an impact on education in the USA. This country with such a vast area and so many natural resources has entrusted the local communities with the control of their schools. Of course, political and historical factors were influential when it was agreed to have locally, rather than centrally controlled schools, but so were the mountain ranges, the rapids, the deserts, and the swamps which separate Washington from the schools in far-flung states.

The nature of the land mass has certainly been one of the determinants of a decentralized system of education in the USA. Decentralization has also been fostered by the love of freedom that grew from the aspirations of the early colonists, and the independent character of their descendants was given new scope after the struggle with the British. Furthermore, the decentralized school system has also been a vehicle (although not always a reliable one) for the pursuit of another 'American dream' — equality of opportunity.

Abundance of mineral and agricultural wealth has provided attractive incentives to students from many of the local school districts. Success has been rewarded with material wealth, and the 'magnetism' of the dollar has been an over-riding influence on individuals and communities. The pursuit of material rewards has also encouraged the adoption of a competitive approach that can be detected in the American way of life, which of course encompasses education.

Independence, freedom, equality, materialism, and competitiveness appear to be some of the national character ingredients effecting the decentralized school system of the USA. It is the teachers at work in this school system who are the clientéle of existing teachers' centres, and so it is interesting to discover what effects these ingredients have had on the teachers and the centres.

In Chapter 7 it was reported that Norwegian teachers' centre leaders had difficulty because teachers reared on a national plan were reluctant to use their own initiative. For different reasons, it seems that many individual American teachers are slow to experiment, even though their country is renowned for technological invention. Paul S. Pilcher suggests that this is because

'There is no history of professional autonomy for teachers in the US. Our schools have been publicly created, publicly owned, and publicly directed'. (Pilcher, 1973)

American school boards have such direct responsibility for the financing of their local schools that they often have a far greater 'say' in what goes on in the classroom. It has earlier been claimed that the autonomy of the English headteachers and of their assistants has resulted in teacher involvement in far-reaching curriculum change, so the lack of autonomy of their American counterpart might have been an impediment to progress.

Bearing in mind that school board officials are constantly seeking local support for their budget proposals, and that reports to the voters contain detailed accounts of how each dollar is spent, it is not surprising that accountability is also a strong influence on curriculum decisions, for the teacher is

'aware of the curriculum innovations that have been banned and the budget fights that have been lost over the issues of teacher permissiveness, social radicalism, and other unpopular sounding causes'. (*ibid.*)

In addition, American teachers have less job security than their 'English cousins', and it is not unheard of for teachers to lose their posts because they have shown individuality.

Parental interest in their children's progress and rights, has accompanied local involvement in educational policy making. In any democratic country it is important that all pupils should be treated fairly, but parental determination that their children should not 'miss out', sometimes leads to a situation in which parent-teacher tension has a deleterious effect —

'The child's every move at school is under constant scrutiny by parents: the grades he receives, the teachers he gets or doesn't get; the special class opportunities he receives or misses; his comprehension of the new math; the incessant questions by parents who are on the look-out night and day for any slippages, any discriminations'. (Bassett, 1970)

Instead of catering for individual differences, teachers are often forced into multiple choice and workbook orientated approaches, if only to make sure that complaints of unfairness cannot be substantiated.

The motivation of many curriculum developers and publishers also springs from a desire for equality. To guard against the effects of poor teaching, efforts have been made to make text books 'teacher proof', but much of this effort emanated from universities and colleges, where specialists devised schemes with little or no consultation with the teachers. In 1970, G. W. Bassett (an Australian) wrote —

'In all this activity for innovation, the dominant figures appear to be the politicians, the professors, the research and curriculum specialists, the engineers, and the publishers, rather than the teachers. The forces working towards change come for the most part from outside the schools'.

Lack of personal involvement prevents the changing of attitudes and can result in lessons that are devoid of excitement and conviction.

Even as teachers' centres have been set up in the USA it seems that educationalists other than classroom teachers have still been well to the fore —

'One looks at the list of participants in a joint-sponsored

teachers' centre conference, and there is an overwhelming preponderance of university and 'curriculum development expert personnel'. The few representatives of school districts turn out to be primarily curriculum supervisors, resource people, etc. One searches in vain, for a few genuine classroom teachers'. (Pilcher, 1973)

A similar observation was made by J. Stuart Maclure, who in *Curriculum Innovation and Practice* (1968) reports that at the Third International Curriculum Conference held in 1967, the English group were heavily weighted with practising teachers, while the American party largely consisted of 'outside experts'.

A further sign of America's lack of faith in the classroom teacher may be seen in the practice of calling in 'consultants' at great expense, whenever problems arise. One disillusioned consultant asserts that — 'The very idea of "instant experts" being able to "fix it" in a few hours a week, seems a purely American fantasy'. (Pilcher, 1973) and Stephen K. Bailey summarizes this state of affairs —

'Few professionals have suffered more painfully and seriously from "being done good to" than teachers. In spite of the fact that they are the ones who work day in and day out on the firing line, the definition of their problems, of their roles, of their goals, always seems to be someone else's responsibility: supervisors, parents, college professors, textbook publishers, self-styled reformers, boards of education, state and national education officials'. (Bailey, 1971)

Not surprisingly, 'being done good to' may have been less productive than '*doing* good'.

Many teachers are also at the receiving end of education, when they participate in university courses to increase their qualifications. The involvement of so many teachers in further study is certainly to be admired, but we should remember that many take part with a view to the increased salary they will receive as credits are amassed, rather than because they wish to improve their professional expertise.

From a much earlier date than in Europe, American universities built up education as a theoretical field of study —

> 'More than any other nation, the United States has tried to build
> a science of instruction, following the lead given by Herbart in
> Germany. This approach has been characterized by a tough
> empiricism, with great attention to variables like amount
> learned and speed of learning, less to qualitative ones like
> personal style'. (Bassett, 1970)

Teachers exposed to such approaches are in strong contrast to
English amateurs who 'muddle through'. However teachers in
England and Norway have shown that they are sceptical of theory
without practice, and in teachers' centres where active
participation is a priority objective, more American teachers may
become confident enough to untie themselves from the
'theoretical apron-strings' of others.

For some observers, a misleading feature of American schooling
is that despite changing curriculum emphases the relationships
within the school have remained informal. Some of this
informality can be attributed to national personality traits and
some to the influence of Dewey and the progressive era, when the
child and society were accorded high status. In the 1950s and
1960s, school relationships remained friendly, but the schools
became more subject and discipline-centred especially after the
successful launching of Sputnik, the importance of which has
already been described.

Sputnik was a Russian 'first' and it had dramatic repercussions
all round the world; in the journal *Phi Delta Kappan* Stephen K.
Bailey described teachers' centres as 'A British First' and the
announcement had a fairly dramatic effect on the American
educational scene —

> 'Amazingly within six to eight months of the appearance of
> Bailey's article, some seventy-five to a hundred teachers' centres
> were in operation in the US'. (Pilcher, 1975)

In addition, the only book on teachers' centres at that time,
Teachers' Centres edited by R. E. Thornbury, became the choice
of the month for an American educational book club. Such a
favourable response is encouraging, but it would be a pity if the

teachers' centre 'bandwagon' was boarded with too little consideration for the *particular* and local needs of the teachers.

b) In operation

In their paper 'Concepts of Teachers' Centres' Bruce R. Joyce
and Marsha Weil divide teachers' centres into three categories —
'the informal', 'the competency based', and 'the corporate'. They
look to England for examples of the 'informal styled' centre,
which they say 'is used to create an environment in which teachers
explore curriculum materials, and help each other think about
approaches to teaching'. (Joyce and Weil, 1973) However,
observers need no longer cross the Atlantic to see such centres in
operation, for in establishments such as the City College Workshop Centre for Open Education in New York City informal
approaches to centre work can daily be witnessed.

Unlike some other more recently set up centres, the Workshop
Centre did not arrive in haste, for it evolved from the College /
school activities led by Professor Lillian Weber from City College.
Having given on-site help to teachers and students, coordinated
the advisory service to Open Corridors, and organized workshop
activities for teachers, Professor Weber then became Director of
this Centre which as its information pamphlet outlines, aims —

> 'to support the professional growth of school people who are
> making changes in the learning environments for children.
> These changes are based on a view that each child learns
> through active and repeated encounters with first hand,
> concrete experiences, through interaction with other people,
> and through reflecting on their experiences and interactions'.

In the face of the re-introduction of subject-centred approaches
following Sputnik, this Harlem Centre is a living example of a
project that has been set up to re-assert the importance of the child
at the centre of the learning process.

Inspired by the writing and reporting of Charles S. Silberman
(1970), and Vincent R. Rogers (1970) and others; excited by visits
to primary schools in England and supported by the work of
Piaget, the campaign for Open Education bears some resemblance
to an election contest. Dr Weber, like colleagues in North Dakota,
Pennsylvania, and California is participating in an educational

crusade to create a fresh climate in American schools. As they venture into 'new territory' they are like the early American pioneers, and as they try to make converts they are like the evangelical ministers. The Open Education advocates also bear comparison with American high pressure salesmen, for like them, they are anxious to attract new customers. Those responsible for the writing of the Centre's prospectus go out of their way to be welcoming, and use a relaxed style that is characteristic of American informality —

'Stop in to relax; bring coffee to make here if you wish. Plan to see a film or slides, refer to our list of available films. It takes only minutes to set up the projectors. Bring a favourite record and use our stereo player. Meet here after class and talk over the good news with us'.

Although the Workshop Centre was founded only in 1972, it has already published many reports. Some of these are part of a public relations exercise, geared at attracting more followers and more finance. Unlike centres in England, which by and large are LEA sponsored, the Harlem Centre receives moral and financial support from various sources. It is sponsored by the New York City Board of Education and City College, but it is funded from federal money released under Title III of the Elementary and Secondary Education Act of 1965. The Centre has also received grants from the Ford Foundation and the Rockefeller Brothers. The federal support is an example of the increased interest that Washington has taken in education in an effort to increase national technological advance and to speed social progress especially in deprived areas where local communities have been unable to make satisfactory educational provision. The Ford and Rockefeller grants are charitable examples of the links between education and American 'big business'.

Businesses of whatever size have to be competitive to be successful, and so had the immigrants who journeyed to the States in search of 'fame and fortune'. National value placed on competition has speeded the progress of students from many poor families, but it has also limited the success of many cooperative ventures. Because of this, at the Harlem and other centres —

'Teachers are encouraged to relate to each other, to rely on each other, and to learn from each other. Such an approach runs counter to the competitive spirit that pervades many of our institutions, not only business-related ones, but others — hospitals, universities, and research centres'. (Evans in Dropkin and Tobier, 1973)

There are strong links between the Harlem Workshop Centre, and educational establishments in England, and it is to be hoped that these links will add to the cooperation for which the Centre is striving.

In the first section in this chapter it was suggested that the lack of classroom teacher involvement in innovative processes had stunted the progress of many projects. Too often, teachers were told what to teach and how to teach it, instead of learning how children learn, by becoming actively involved in one's own learning. At the Workshop Centre the emphasis is on 'doing', for through action it is hoped that the attitudes of the teachers, and not just the content of the lessons will be changed. One Centre participant reported —

'The experiences I have had at the Centre have opened a whole new way of teaching to me. I feel that I am finally reaching the children in ways I never thought possible. I feel more secure about myself as a teacher; more able to take initiative, to explore. These feelings extended into my personal life as well. The Centre has been very important to me'. (Chittendon *et al.*, 1973)

This teacher's repeated reference to feelings show that for her at least, the Centre has been able to extend its influence into the affective domain, and this must surely be a commendable achievement for a teachers' centre, or any other establishment concerned with education.

Even though the Workshop Centre has been described because it is an example of an 'informal styled' centre, we have already seen that it has some of the characteristics of Joyce and Weil's 'competency-based centres'. For, as a recipient of federal and foundation finance, it has been obliged to provide evidence that it is 'good value for money'. The First Evaluative Study of the Centre was made by the Education Testing Service from Princeton, New

Jersey, which used questionnaire and interview devices, in order
to measure the extent to which the Centre is fulfilling its
objectives.

This emphasis on the competency of teachers and teachers'
centres is in keeping with the national desire of Americans to test,
score, check, standardize and evaluate, which has often had a
restricting influence on teachers' initiative —

'Accountability is Washington's latest discovery. As a result, the
USOE has insisted upon a set of academically rigorous performance criteria for teachers' centres, necessitating a certain
amount of research expertise not possessed by most teachers.
Classroom teachers are thus barred from meaningful participation in a variety of ways. One might well ask what happened
to the original idea of a local site set up by teachers to meet their
particular needs working as professionals'.

Even in the 'informal styled' Workshop Centre there seems to be a
lack of teacher involvement in the decision making, so it is to be
hoped that as teachers' centres in England become more concerned with evaluation, teacher initiative will not be curtailed.

An example of the American 'competency-based' centre is the
Texas Triple T. Project which is trying to find out

'how we build a teacher education program in Texas,
beginning the day a person decides to enter the teaching
profession until he or she retires, that places ability ahead of a
somewhat sterile collection of semester hours or a specific
number of training hours.' (Joyce and Weil, 1973)

In an attempt to progress towards this goal, the Project has
developed management systems which monitor the effectiveness
of original and redesigned training programmes. At first, the
strengths and teachers are diagnosed, and according to the
diagnosis varying modules are prescribed, and these are generally
made up of specialist training. Rediagnosis then follows, and the
effectiveness of the process is ascertained.

At another 'competency-based' centre attached to Clark
University, behavioural modification techniques connected with
the classroom are again used, but teachers also participate in
curriculum development and educational research. The staff of

the centre is made up of educational technicians, psychologists, lawyers, and members of community action groups, so that behavioural as well as curriculum problems are considered. Some of the 'competency-based' centres make use of micro-teaching facilities, and it would seem that the use of these techniques could be considerably extended in British pre- and in-service educational establishments.

Just as some teachers' centres share 'informal' and 'competency-based' characteristics, so also do they possess some features of the 'corporate' centres. Whereas the 'informal' centres owe much to the English models, and the 'competency-based' centres have been strongly influenced by the American 'educational measurement' movement, the 'corporate styled' centre has its origins in the workings of 'big business'. For example,

'The Central Administration of the Montgomery County Schools operates from a plan developed by the management consultants Booz, Allen and Hamilton, which serves big corporations more frequently than educational groups'. (Joyce and Weil, 1973)

Through the scheme workshops and in-service training courses are provided, together with a consultancy service, and a micro-teaching laboratory. In the centre which coordinates the project, university staff and pre- and in-service teachers are brought together as also are materials from which curriculum development activities might spring.

In Maryland, fifty elementary and secondary schools are involved in a 'corporate' enterprise, which strongly resembles the professional centre model proposed by Lord James. In the middle of the scheme, are coordinators, who are paid equally by the School Boards and the Colleges. Each coordinator is responsible for students in initial training and for the in-service education of the staff in the schools involved. These coordinators are like full-time 'professional tutors' and

'The centre idea implies sets of students working with sets of teachers working with sets of lecturers all at different levels of experience, helping one another to learn more about teaching'.

Some problems faced at this centre in Maryland are described by Leon Boucher in a *Trends in Education* article. He says that there is sometimes role conflict when headteachers and coordinators do not agree, and there are financial problems connected with the running of centre premises shared by the schools and the colleges. In England all professional centres will be financed by the LEAs, so the accommodation problem should not arise here, but it is likely that much will have to be done to avoid tension between headteachers, heads of departments, and professional tutors.

In the first part of this chapter it was suggested that in the USA, the vastness of the country had encouraged the development of a decentralized system of education, within which great variation exists. This variety is clearly exemplified in teachers' centres where there is little certainty about what a centre might look like or what it might do. However, just as the Schools Council has provided some common denominators to the evolving centres in England and Wales and as the National Conference of Teachers' Centre Leaders (NCTCL) has given unity, so may the National Education Association influence the development of some pattern in the USA. The NEA has issued a Briefing Memo called 'In-service Education and Teachers' Centres', a paper called 'Teacher Centred Professional Development', and a document entitled 'What a Teachers' Centre might look like', and in the latter there appears a description, which for a land of initiative, experiment, enterprise, and progressive ideas, should provide a foundation on which to build

'A teachers' centre should be an accessible physical setting serving a cluster of schools, developed and managed by the teacher clientele, containing appropriate spaces, material, equipment and staff for the purpose of encouraging and supporting effective and meaningful professional development which will lead to improved educational opportunities for students'. (Hyer *et al., nd*)

Chapter 9

Teacher Advisory Centres in a developing country — Kenya

In 1974 there were forty-two teacher advisory centres in Kenya. All districts except one had a centre, and some had two. They have been established by the government to speed the Primary Schools' Supervisory Service Scheme, which was started in 1969 with the assistance of UNICEF. Centres are led by centre tutors, who are recommended for the appointments by the district education officer, and the school inspectors.

Mr B. D. Odhiambo (1974) suggests that the centres will improve the quality of Kenyan education by

(a) 'Offering in-service courses to primary school teachers in urban and rural areas,

(b) Being a major contact point between the teacher in the district and various educational institutions in the country,

(c) Giving support in effecting processes of educational change,

(d) Contributing towards the National Curriculum Development

and

(e) Informing the Society of what is expected of them in educational reform.'

It seems that Kenya has a similar problem to Norway, in that just as the needs of Oslo and the fjords are totally different, so are there vast differences between schools in Nairobi and those in the remote rural areas. The teacher advisory centres aim to facilitate a more even spread of education improvement, and in some areas it is proposed to set up 'sub-centres' linked to 'mother centres' so that distance between the teacher and centre can be reduced. Furthermore, it is suggested that the provision of specially equipped vehicles will enable centre facilities to be taken to the schools.

'Big districts with few schools will need more hardy vehicles with less petrol consumption e.g. long wheel base landrover. Small districts with higher school population would do very well with three ton lorries or Volkswagen Kombis'. (*ibid.*)

In his *Study of Curriculum Development in Kenya* (1972) Gordon Bessey suggested that one of the most urgent needs was for teachers in isolated areas to be made aware of new publications, and so the journeys of these 'mobile units' should help to alleviate this need. Mobile and permanent units also help solve problems caused by lack of resources in the schools. Teachers can use at the centres, or borrow for use in their own schools, equipment that is too costly for individual schools to purchase.

One of the centres' aims is to improve the material resources of the schools, and one of the tasks of the centre tutors is to improve the standard of teaching in the schools. To help with this second objective, each teacher advisory centre is linked with at least five schools that are within a five mile radius. These 'example schools' are frequently visited by the centre tutors who act as supervisors to all members of staff. Their job is to give professional advice, to help teachers overcome their weaknesses, and to keep a record of each teachers' progress. These 'example schools' follow the official curriculum, but teachers are encouraged to make adaptations according to local circumstances. It is suggested that when progress has been made, the centre tutors should start work in new 'example schools', and enlist the help of teachers in the original schools in the running of 'in-service courses'. Through this systematic staff improvement process, which resembles the network proposed by the Schools Council 'Progress in Learning

Science' project (Harlen, 1974) mentioned in Chapter 5, it is hoped that centre tutors will play a part in the quickening of educational progress in Kenya.

Despite the implementation of policies to speed the movement of educational advances from central areas to outlying districts, it is recognized that central provision needs to be strengthened. Because of this, the Ministry of Education suggests that

'There will be a need to establish a Central Educational Resource and Advisory Centre at KIE — Nairobi, because this is where curriculum development and research work is carried out, and besides, it is centrally situated in this country'. (*ibid.*)

The centre would provide a meeting place for a wide variety of educationalists and facilities for the production of curriculum materials.

Already Kenya has plans for a highly developed network of teacher advisory centres, and it is apparent that her decision-makers, encouraged by the teachers' centre kits produced by the British Council, have great confidence in these establishments. The Kenyan Centre's aims are in line with those of teachers' centres in many other countries, but in this rapidly emerging country, where many may be impatient for progress, decision makers will do well to heed this straightforward advice from Gordon Bessey (1972): 'The contribution of teachers of whatever status must be seen as important if the scheme is to be successful'.

Chapter 10

In Conclusion

Since the James Report was published, the Arabs and Israelis have been at war, the rate of inflation has escalated dramatically, and 'the prophets of doom' have moved to the 'centre of the arena'. Consequently, in spite of the general support that greeted the Report, it is now taken for granted that Third Cycle activities will not now be extended to anything like the amount envisaged by Lord James. As Professor R. Webster (a member of the Report Committee) said in an interview reported by Silver (1975): 'Now it looks pretty bleak to get money for Cycle III because it is the one thing that the LEAs can easily drop'. In fact, although the facilities of teachers' centres have been used to attract teachers to their schools, LEAs have shown that they 'can easily drop' teachers' centres also. A few centres have already been 'axed', some are awaiting news of their future, and some have had their expenditure and staffing reduced.

In the first edition of *Centre* (Ed. Cartwright, 1975), the former newsletter of the National Conference of Teachers' Centre Leaders (NCTCL) we are told — 'Clearly the development of teachers' centres as advocated by all major educational reports since the early sixties is in jeopardy'. Harry Kahn (former Secretary of the National Conference of Teachers' Centre Leaders) drew the attention of a wider readership to the possible demise of teachers' centres in a 1975 *Times Educational Supplement* article entitled 'Save our Teachers' Centres'. In December 1976 under the heading 'Where the next axe may fall' a reporter for the same newspaper predicted that —

'In-service training will probably be an early casualty and many teachers' centres may find the scope of their activities considerably reduced, some may even be closed, but large scale closures are not expected'.

It seems that those involved in teachers' centre work may have to divert some of their time and energy towards preservation, if these establishments are to be no more than 'passing fancies'.

Some centres have already been closed, but in many areas, for example West Berkshire, teachers have not let their strong support for *their* centres go unnoticed. A suggestion (not a proposal) that the closure of the teachers' centre in Newbury could save the local authority £9,000 resulted in the holding of protest meetings, the signing of petitions, and the writing of letters expressing grave concern at such a course of action. Local newspapers contained the headlines such as 'Teachers unite to oppose Closure', and this unity resulted in a later article under the heading 'Reprieve for Teachers' Centre' which announced that the closure suggestion would not be acted on at present. Similarly in Leicestershire a massive campaign by both teachers and other concerned parties has recently saved Crown Hill House Centre in Leicester and a Centre at Blaby in the south of the County. (*The Teacher*, 1976) Such positive and immediate action by so many teachers is an indication that there is strong 'grassroot' support for the retention of teachers' centres, even at a time of drastic cuts in educational expenditure.

However, despite the widespread acknowledgement that teachers' centres deserve a place on the educational map, it may well be that in order to 'Save the Centres', sacrifices will have to be made, if only for a limited period. At present, many teachers' centres offer 'fringe' in-service courses such as pottery and guitar playing. If these are to continue it may be expedient for enrolment fees to be levied. Additionally, it may be necessary to arrange more in-service courses during vacation periods. We have already seen how many teachers would be prepared to use centres in the vacations, so the organization of holiday courses would not only answer this request but also save money on replacement staff. Making more use of teachers' centres and other educational establishments during vacation periods would also make more economic use of valuable publicly owned 'real estate'. Now that many schools have a longer winter break in order to cut fuel bills, the first week of January may be a suitable time for such courses.

In the *Bulletin for Environmental Education* published by the Town and Country Planning Association, another way of making more economic use of teachers' centres is suggested — 'a variant on the Schools Council Information Section idea in the form of an Urban Studies Centre, catering for pupils as well as teachers'. Teachers' centres are not always fully used during school hours, and many have indoor and outdoor environments that contain many 'springboards' for study. Similarly other centres may be advised to follow the example set by the Maths Centre at Stapleford (Stone, 1975) where classes of children can be introduced to a whole range of mathematical experiences while their teachers are free to explore the learning materials on display. By encouraging pupils as well as teachers to use the centres for learning based on direct experience, the pupils' study may be made more meaningful, and the teachers' attitude towards curriculum change may be influenced by active involvement instead of merely listening to the exhortations of 'earlier converts'.

If teachers' centres become study centres for rural-urban-environmental studies and workshops for pupil actitivities, not only would their premises be in operation to give a more economic return for the cost of upkeep, but so also might more secondary school colleagues be persuaded to become involved in centre work. In *Lost for Words* (1973) Patrick Creber accurately described the existing situation —

> 'Too few centres at present are well supported by staff in both primary and secondary schools, some have had particular difficulty in engaging the interest of secondary teachers'.

Many of Lord James' proposals for First and Second Cycle activities were designed to break down some of the barriers that exist within the teaching profession, and so if teachers' centres become less exclusively used by primary school colleagues, the James Committee's criticism of 'the divisiveness which has bedevilled the teaching profession for so many years' will be removed. It is because teachers in primary schools are generally attempting to improve their expertise over a whole range of curricular areas, that they more frequently experience the need to become involved in teachers' centre activities. Through involvement they often become committed to the work of the teachers' centre. Secondary colleagues on the other hand have more resources within their own schools, and they also work in more confined subject areas. Consequently they less frequently feel the need to call upon the services of the teachers' centre, and so their commitment to its work has often been less serious.

Although teachers' centres may try to eliminate some of the 'divisiveness' in education, the James recommendations on professional centres could lead to the formation of different divisions. If only the very large and geographically well-suited centres become professional centres or part of a professional centre 'network', a 'two tier' system could easily emerge. This might result in the smaller institutions being involved only in low status activities, which would rarely appeal to secondary school colleagues.

One result of the implementation of Lord James' recommendations for the First Cycle, would be that teachers will receive the preparation for their careers in the company of contemporaries not planning a teaching career. As was shown in Chapter 4 of this study, teachers' centres are increasingly being used by non-teachers who are engaged in youth and community work, and in the Social Services. If this trend continues teachers' centres may help to implement one of the James' Report's main aims — to solve 'the problem of isolation'.

Besides showing teachers' centres as meeting places for teachers and non-teachers, Chapter 4 also gave details of teachers' centres acting as resource centres. The building up of resources has often happened naturally as teaching and learning materials have been needed for activities at the centre. Useful though these resources are, the limited range of items that a small establishment can offer, highlights the need for a more centralized and professional approach to this educational service. Constantly used resources need to be kept at hand in the schools, materials of a strictly local nature seem best stored at the teachers' centres, but more regional centres within a national system could provide a comprehensive service that would be uneconomic in a smaller unit. Problems of immediate availability, and efficient communication quickly spring to mind, but surely our improved telephone system, and the apparently limitless potential of computers could be taken advantage of to avoid the duplication and waste of effort that seems likely in the near future. As so many arguments are now won largely on grounds of economy, the rationalization of resource provision, and maybe the increase of expenditure on technical help to give greater return for investment on educational hardware, could convince the decision-makers that teachers' centres are a vital money saver rather than a 'fringe benefit'.

One of the pressing problems facing teachers' centres especially in rural areas is the spiralling cost of petrol which discourages colleagues from making long journeys. LEAs continue in most cases to re-imburse teachers for the travel expenses connected with course attendance, but there is still the problem of expenditure incurred in making informal visits to the centres. Regional delivery systems are also expensive, so there seems to be a need for more radical improvization. It is even possible that a converted double-decker bus could become a travelling teachers' centre — with one section being used as a base for a loan service, and another to act as a meeting place for on-site curriculum meetings! It would also be sensible for conveniently located teachers' centres to liaise more closely so that more shared use can be made of resources. Some equipment may only be needed in one place intermittently, so planned purchasing could help gain maximum return for investment.

Many English teachers' centres grew up and flourished in the Sixties because they had spontaneity, independence, and idealism that generated enthusiasm and commitment. They thrived on the same sort of dedication that filled the newly designed primary schools where the original and generally 'hand-picked' staff members strove to make the schools a success. Just as the 'honeymoon' for many of these schools is now over, and head-teachers struggle to keep alive the same spirit as staff leave, and are replaced by colleagues with less conviction, so also is the 'honeymoon' now over for most teachers' centres. The question asked by Mr W. G. Hamflett at the Schools Council Regional Study Conference held at Matlock in 1972, still needs to be answered —

'how can they grow beyond what in many instances are separate cottage industries without losing that essential element of real belonging to teachers, and the area they serve'?

If the centres become part of the Jamesian professional centre network, recognition may give them new maturity, but there is a danger that 'institutionalizing the concept will kill the concept' (Greenwood in Thornbury (Ed.), 1973a) — for then the 'cottage industries' would become 'curriculum development factories' that could improve productivity but lose sight of the children in the classrooms.

Similar dangers are contained both in the provision of teachers' centre recipes for use in developing countries such as Kenya and in the setting up of teachers' centres in the USA by educationalists who have been excited by visits to centres in England. Teachers' centres are often used as agencies for change, but especially in age of instant solutions we would do well to remember —

'that any attempt, no matter how thorough and deliberate, to use education as an immediate remedy to change an existing culture pattern is bound to fail'. (Mallinson, 1975)

In spite of this reservation there is no doubt that much of the experimentation and expansion of the Sixties has given way to the evaluation and accountability of the Seventies. For a long time many organizers of in-service provision have relied upon teacher response and informal feedback to judge whether activities have been worthwhile. However, an increasing number of attempts are now being made to find more reliable methods of checking whether courses are achieving the hoped-for results. For example, Bernard Crix (1976), the Warden of Southend Teachers' Centre, has described how Bloom's taxonomy (1956) was used to assess the effectiveness of courses held at the centre. Mr Crix recognizes the limitations of the evaluation method used but it does provide a framework by means of which courses that have clearly definable objectives may be evaluated. Bloom's taxonomy was used by Mr Crix to evaluate courses on 'Examinations and Assessment', 'First Aid', and 'Educational Objectives', but another writer (Henderson, 1976) has described how techniques for the measurement of attitudes were used with colleagues attending courses on a seemingly less measurable subject — 'Pastoral Care'. Once again reservations are made about the success of the study but among the conclusions is a finding that has significance for leaders of establishments such as teachers' centres that are largely concerned with part-time in-service work —

'sustained attitude change is more likely to arise from part-time
than from full-time training, possibly because of the absence of
conflicting frames of reference'.

— for at a time when all forms of in-service education are being
'put under the microscope' especially with regard to cost-effective-
ness, teachers' centres which rarely offer full-time courses may be
encouraged in their efforts aimed at attitude change.

During the years when teachers' centre provision was being
extended, an increasing degree of interest was being shown in
education by members of the general public. This interest
together with many criticisms culminated in the eventual invitation from the Prime Minister, Mr Callaghan, for the country to
take part in an Education Debate, for which an annotated agenda
(DES, 1976) has been prepared. The Debate has national
significance but the outcome should have local implications, and
it may be that teachers' centres which have been dedicated to the
localizing of national issues and projects, will be well equipped to
help implement any agreed changes. For example, the Debate has
already shown that there is a need for more liaison between
schools and industry, and it is possible that teachers' centres will
be able to help forge links between school and local industries for
the mutual benefit of all.

The teachers' centre movement gathered momentum at the
same time as the colleges of education were responding to the cries
for more teachers, and when the schools were coping with a rising
child population. This state of affairs was short-lived and colleges
are now being phased out, and schools are re-adjusting to take in
fewer new entrants because of the decline in the birth rate. The
advantages and disadvantages of rapid teacher turnover are being
replaced by the advantages and disadvantages of staff stability.
The new state of affairs should enable consolidation to take place,
but there are also dangers of stagnation and a lowering of morale.
In this new situation it would seem that there is great scope for
teachers' centres to introduce dynamism into the system and
provide opportunities for continuing professional renewal.

In spite of changed circumstances especially with regard to
finance, there have been repeated pleas for the continuation of in-

service education so that the quality of education can be improved. Accompanying these pleas has been the realization that teacher education is not just a matter of injecting some new expertise here or of collecting a new diploma there, but rather that it is a life-long process. As teachers' centres are sited in the community served by the schools, and are made credible by their accessibility and their responsiveness to change, it would seem that they have a vital role to play in this life-long process. Desirable though it may be for a teacher to attend a course at College X or Resort Y, situated 150 miles from their school, the possibilities for 'after-care' would seem minimal. On the other hand the close proximity of a local teachers' centre should make professional 're-fuelling' and 'servicing' more appropriate and long-lasting.

Although teachers' centres have a relatively short history, and are as yet far from adequately documented, it seems that they have already been strongly influenced by national characteristics. In Norway, which has a fairly centralized school system Pedagogic Centres have been set up to speed the implementation of government policy. In the USA the variety of teachers' centres is indicative of the freedom that exists within a decentralized system, but their dependence of colleges and universities is evidence of the limited autonomy of teachers in the schools. When we turn to our own country it seems that even now after such a short period of teachers' centre history, Sir Michael Sadler's claim that 'Great Britain is one of the bridges between East and West' (cited by Mallinson, 1975) is being illustrated. For our teachers' centre network is neither controlled by a national council as in Norway, or dependent on private institutions as in the USA. However a national council is on the way, and cutbacks in LEA spending on teachers' centres may force them to look elsewhere for financial support. Whatever changes lie ahead, whether they result from the James Report's recommendations, the economic crisis, or the Great Education Debate it would seem that increased teacher and community involvement in teachers' centres in England and Wales will help them to survive, and to act as models for patient observers from other countries.

APPENDIX

Basic details of five teachers' centres in *one* **re-organized LEA to show variety of accommodation and staffing**

Centre 1

a) Situation — Purpose designed terrapin type building in grounds of primary school.

b) Accommodation — Practical room, lecture room, office, dark room, discussion room, hall.

c) Area served — Fairly large town, and widely scattered area.

d) Antecedents — Advisory service base with Nuffield French bias/teachers' centre in different part of district.

e) Leader's title — Warden (part-time).

f) Leader's salary scale — Scale 3.

g) Other staff — Part-time secretary.

Centre 2

a) Situation — Ground floor and part of first floor of former Victorian residence.

b) Accommodation — Office, lecture room, lounge, resources room, workshop, work-kitchens, storeroom, meeting room, reading unit.

c) Area served — Three fairly large towns, and the surrounding villages.

d) Antecedents — Advisory teachers' room.

e) Former use of premises — Private residence, boys' home, secondary school annexe, drama groups' rehearsal rooms.

f) Leader's title — Warden.

g) Leader's Salary scale — Head teacher Group 4 school.

h) Other staff — Part-time secretary.
Part-time resources assistant
Part-time technical assistant.

Centre 3

a) Situation — First floor section within comprehensive school.

b) Accommodation — Lecture room, committee room, office, reprographic area, practical area, shared refreshment area.

c) Area served — Two towns and surrounding villages, plus large suburban area.

d) Antecedents — ROSLA unit.

e) Former use of premises — Secondary school classrooms.

f) Leader's title — Director.

g) Leader's salary scale — Head teacher Group 4 school.

h) Other staff — Shared technician
Part-time secretary.

Centre 4

a) Situation — Two storey block in grounds of primary school.

b) Accommodation — Conference room, office, reprographic room, craft workshop, two discussion rooms, practical lecture room.

c) Area served — Very large town.

d) Antecedents — Nuffield Mathematics Centre.

e) Former use of premises — Secondary school craft / home economics block.

f) Leader's title — Warden.

g) Leader's salary scale — Head teacher Group 5 school.

h) Other staff — Part-time secretary
Part-time general assistant
Full-time technician.

Centre 5

a) Situation — Four double HORSA units in grounds of primary school.

b) Accommodation — Three meeting rooms, two work rooms, office and canteen, audiovisual aids store, resource room.

c) Area served — Very large town.

d) Antecedents — Nuffield Mathematics Centre.

e) Former use of premises — Primary school classrooms.

f) Leader's title — Director.

g) Leader's salary scale — Head teacher Group 5 school.

h) Other staff — Resources advisory officer, two part-time secretaries, part-time technician.

REFERENCES

ADAMS, E. (Ed) (1975). *In-Service Education and Teachers' Centres*. Oxford: Pergamon Press.

ASHTON, P., DAVIES, F., KNEEN, P. (1975) *Aims into Practice in the Primary School*. London: Hodder and Stoughton.

BAILEY, S. K. (1971). 'Teachers' centres: a British first', *Phi Delta Kappan*, 53, 3, 146—9.

BAKER, K. and BOLAM, R. (1976). 'Helping new teachers: the induction year', *D.E.S. Reports on Education No. 84*.

BASSETT, G. W. (1970). *Innovation in Primary Education*. London: John Wiley.

BELL, R. and PRESCOTT, W. (Eds) (1975). *The Schools Council: A Second Look*. London: Ward Lock Educational.

BERESFORD, C. (1974). 'Teachers' centre processes and in-service opportunities', *Cambridge J. of Educ.*, 4, 2, 93—101.

BESSEY, G. D. *et al.* (1972). *A Study of Curriculum Development in Kenya*. Nairobi: Ministry of Education.

BIRCHENOUGH, C. (1938). *History of Elementary Education in England and Wales from 1800 to the Present day*. (3rd Edit) London: Tutorial Press.

BLOOM, B. S. (Ed) (1956) *Taxonomy of Educational Objectives Handbook I*. Cognitive domain. Harlow: Longman.

BLYTH, A., DERRICOTT, R., ELLIOTT, G., SUMMER, H., and WAPLINGTON, A. (1975). *Place, Time and Society, 8—13; an introduction*. Bristol: Collins.

BOARD OF EDUCATION (1944). *Report of Committee appointed to consider the supply, recruitment, and training of teachers, and youth leaders*. (McNair Report). London: HMSO.

BOLAM, R. (1973). *Induction Programmes for Probationary Teachers*. Research Unit, University of Bristol School of Education.

BOUCHER, L. (1971). 'A centre in Maryland, U.S.A,' *Trends in Education*, 23, 46—7.

BRADLEY, H., FLOOD, P., and PADFIELD, T, (1975). 'What do we want for teachers' centres?', *Brit. J. of In-Service Educ.*, 1, 3, 41—8.

BRAITHWAITE, J. (1971). *Teachers' Centres*. Unpublished Schools' Council paper(mimeographed).

CAMDEN WESTMINSTER TEACHERS' CENTRE (1974). Courses for September / October — Newsletter Part 2.

CANE, B. (1969). *In-service Training — a study of Teachers' Views and Preferences*. Slough: NFER.

CARTWRIGHT, J. (Ed) (1975a). *Centre: Newsletter of the NCTCL*, No. 1, January 1975. National Conference of Teachers' Centre Leaders.

CARTWRIGHT, J. (Ed) (1975b). *Centre: Newsletter of the NCTCL*, No. 2, July 1975.

CARTWRIGHT, J. (Ed) (1976). *Centre: Newsletter of the NCTCL*, No. 3, February 1976.

CAVE, R. G. (1971). *An Introduction to Curriculum Development*. London: Ward Lock Educational.

CHILDS, G. F. P., SMITH, R., DAVIDSON, M. and BRAITHWAITE, P. A. (1972). 'Teachers' centres: A vital and evolving educational service', *Visual Education*, October, 41—51.

CHITTENDEN, E., BUSSIS, A. M., AMAREL, M., KIM, N. and GODSHALK, M. H. (1973). First Year Evaluative Study of the Workshop Centre for Open Education, City College of New York (mimeographed).

CHRISTIAN, G. A. (1922). *English Education from Within*. London: Wallace Gandy.

CREBER, P. (1973) *Lost for Words*. London: Penguin Books in Association with NATE.

CRIX, B. (1976). 'Objectives and the evaluation of in-service education courses viewed in the light of 'Bloom's Taxonomy', *Brit. J. of In-Service Educ.*, **2**, 2, 106—11.

CULLING, G. (1974). 'Introduction to the teachers' centre', *Educational Development International*, **2**, 1.

CURRY, A. (1968). 'The organization of a teachers' centre: Spring Bank Teachers' Centre, Leeds', *Visual Education*, Dec., 10—2.

DALE, I. R. and TAYLOR, J. K. (1971). A National Survey of Teachers in their First Year of Service. Research Unit, University of Bristol School of Education.

DEPARTMENT OF EDUCATION AND SCIENCE: CENTRAL ADVISORY COUNCIL FOR EDUCATION (ENGLAND) (1963). *Half our Future* (Newsom Report). London: HMSO.

DEPARTMENT OF EDUCATION AND SCIENCE: CENTRAL ADVISORY COUNCIL FOR EDUCATION (ENGLAND) (1967). *Children and their Primary Schools*. (Plowden Report) London: HMSO.

DEPARTMENT OF EDUCATION AND SCIENCE: CENTRAL ADVISORY COUNCIL FOR EDUCATION (WALES) (1967). *Primary Education in Wales*. (Gittens Report). London: HMSO.

DEPARTMENT OF EDUCATION AND SCIENCE (1972). *Teacher Education and Training*. (James Report). London: HMSO.

DEPARTMENT OF EDUCATION AND SCIENCE (1972). *Education: a Frame-work for Expansion*. (Govt. White Paper). London: HMSO.

DEPARTMENT OF EDUCATION AND SCIENCE: CENTRAL ADVISORY COUNCIL FOR EDUCATION (ENGLAND) (1975). *A Language for Life*. (Bullock Report). London: HMSO.

DEPARTMENT OF EDUCATION AND SCIENCE: ADVISORY COMMITTEE ON THE SUPPLY AND TRAINING OF TEACHERS (1974). Sub-Committee on Induction and In-Service Training: Some considerations (mimeographed).

DEPARTMENT OF EDUCATION AND SCIENCE: ADVISORY COMMITTEE ON THE SUPPLY AND TRAINING OF TEACHERS (1975). Sub-Committee on Induction and In-Service Training. Discussion Paper on INSET Provision (mimeographed).

DEPARTMENT OF EDUCATION AND SCIENCE: ADVISORY COMMITTEE ON THE SUPPLY AND TRAINING OF TEACHERS (1976). Report by the Induction and In-Service Sub-Committee. Towards a National Policy for the Induction and In-Service Training of Teachers in Schools (mimeographed).

DEPARTMENT OF EDUCATION AND SCIENCE: ADVISORY COMMITTEE ON THE SUPPLY AND TRAINING OF TEACHERS (1976). Report of Working Party set up by Sub-Committee on Induction and In-Service Training. The Contribution of Colleges and Departments of Education to INSET. (mimeographed).

DEPARTMENT OF EDUCATION AND SCIENCE (1976). Schools in England and Wales: current issues; an annotated agenda for discussion.

DIXON, W. (1965). *Society Schools and Progress in Scandinavia*. Oxford: Pergamon.

DROPKIN, R. and TOBIER, A. (Eds.) (1973). Notes from Workshop Centre for Open Education, New York, **2**, 2, 20 (mimeographed).

EDMONDS, E. L. (1958). 'S.P.C.K. and early inspection of Anglican Church schools', *Studies in Education*, **3**, 1, 50—9.

EDUCATIONAL SUPPLY ASSOCIATION (1960). Approaches to Science in the Primary School.

ERAUT, M. (1972). *In-Service Education for Innovation.* Occasional Paper 4. National Council for Educational Technology.

EXETER UNIVERSITY, SCHOOL OF EDUCATION (1974). Regional Resources Centre. Information Leaflet.

GODDARD, D. (1976). The role of the Teachers' Centre in school-focussed INSET. Unpublished discussion paper prepared for the conference 'Providing school focussed INSET — who is involved?' held at Institute of Education. University of London 1976 (mimeographed).

GOODACRE, E. J. (1975). 'Teachers' Centres and Provision for Reading — including a Directory of Reading Centres'. Centre for the Teaching of Reading, School of Education, University of Reading (mimeographed).

HARLEN, W. (1964) Progress in Learning Science Information Paper No. 3. London: Schools Council. (mimeographed).

HENDERSON, E. S. (1975). 'The extent of teachers' involvement in in-service training', *Brit. J. of In-Service Educ.,* 2, 1, 29—33 and 54.

HENDERSON, E. S. (1976). 'Attitude change in in-service training', *Brit. J. of In-Service Educ.,* 2, 2, 113—6.

HILL, D. (1975) 'Experiments in induction: new approaches to the probationary year', *Brit. J. of Teacher Educ.,* 1, 1, 29—40.

HILSUM, J. (1976). Victoria's Island — a case study of a local history project. Isle of Wight Teachers' Centre (unpublished paper) (mimeographed).

HOLLICK, E. J. (1972). A study of the in-service training of primary school teachers with particular reference to teacher contributions to teachers' centres. Unpublished Special Study, University of London, Institute of Education.

HYER, A. L. KNISPEL, M. R., LUKE, R. A., and MCCLURE, R. M. 'What a Teacher Centre might look like'. Washington DC: National Education Association (mimeographed).

INTERSKOLA (1973). Report of Sixth International Conference on Education in sparsely populated countries (Alta — Norway — July 18—25th 1973)

JOHNSTON, D. J. (1971). *Teachers' In-Service Education.* Oxford: Pergamon Press.

JOYCE, R. and WEIL, M. (1973). *Concepts of Teachers' Centres* (microfiche). Washington D.C.: ERIC: Clearinghouse on Teacher Education.

KAHN, H. (1975). 'Save our teachers' centres', *Times Educ. Suppl.*, 3 1 4 8, 2.

LAWRENCE, G, (1975). 'In-service teaching — what the teachers want', *Brit. J. of In-Service Educ.*, 1, 2, 49—53.

LEEDS UNIVERSITY, INSTITUTE OF EDUCATION (1973). *The Objectives of Teacher Education.* Slough: NFER.

LIGHT, A. J. (1975). 'Teachers, experts and curriculum change', *Dialogue*, 19, 8—9.

LIVERPOOL EDUCATION COMMITTEE (1975). Pilot Scheme for the Induction of New Teachers. (Report No. 1) Organisation (mimeographed).

LIVERPOOL EDUCATION COMMITTEE (1975). Pilot Scheme for the Induction of New Teachers. (Report No. 2) Appointment of Teacher Tutors. (mimeographed)

LIVERPOOL EDUCATION COMMITTEE (1975). Pilot Scheme for the Induction of New Teachers. (Report No. 3). Briefing of Teacher Tutors. (mimeographed).

LIVERPOOL EDUCATION COMMITTEE (1975). Pilot Scheme for the Induction of New Teachers. (Report No. 4). Release of New Teachers to follow Induction Programmes (mimeographed).

LIVERPOOL EDUCATION COMMITTEE (1975). Pilot Scheme for the Induction of New Teachers. (Report No. 5). Induction Programmes for New Teachers. (mimeographed).

MACLURE, J. S. (Ed) (1968). *Curriculum Innovation in Practice.* Report of Third International Curriculum Conference 1967. London: HMSO.

MCGEENEY, P. and YOUNG, M. (1968). *Learning Begins at Home.* London: Routledge & Kegan Paul.

MALLINSON, V. (1975). *An Introduction to the Study of Comparative Education.* (4th Edition). London: Heinemann.

MARTINEAU TEACHERS' CLUB (1955). 'Focus on Birmingham,' *Education,* 105, 402—3.

THE MATHEMATICAL ASSOCIATION (1955). *The Teaching of Mathematics in the Primary School.* London: Bell.

MINISTRY OF EDUCATION (1961) *Science in the Primary School.* Pamphlet No. 42. London: HMSO.

NATIONAL UNION OF TEACHERS (1972). A survey of centre resources and conditions of service of leaders. London: NUT.

NICHOLS, C. A. and WEEKS, L. H. (1975). 'In-service training — teachers' preferences today', *Brit. J. of In-Service Educ.*, 1, 2, 26—9.

NORTH AND EAST MIDLANDS WARDENS AND UNIVERSITY OF NOTTINGHAM SCHOOL OF EDUCATION (1972). Report of the Second National Conference of Wardens/Leaders of Teachers' Centres: Held at the University of Nottingham. April 1972. (mimeographed).

ODHIAMBO, B. D. (1974). The Teacher Advisory Centres. Brief prepared for Kenyan Ministry of Education Inspectorate (mimeographed).

OWEN, J. G. (1972). 'Developing teachers' centres', *Trends in Education*, **28**, 2—7.

OWEN, J. G. (1973). *The Management of Curriculum Development*. Cambridge: Cambridge Univ. Press.

PILCHER, P. S. (1973). 'Teacher centres: can they work here?', *Phi Delta Kappan*, **54**, 340—3.

POLLARD, M. (1970). 'Soft centres in in-service training', *Education and Training*, **12**, 380—1 and 386.

PRICE, G. (1973). 'How the James Professional Centres might work', *Times Higher Educ. Suppl.*, **68**, 14.

RICHARDS, C. (1972). 'Teachers' centres — a primary school view', *Trends in Education*, **25**, 31—3.

RICHARDS, F. (1975). 'Mathematics inside a multi-purpose teachers' centre', *Mathematics Teaching* **72**, 28—9.

ROBERTS, I. F. (1975). 'Chemistry teachers' centres', *Education in Chemistry*, **12**, 76—7.

ROGERS, V. R. (Ed) (1970). *Teaching in the British Primary School*. London: Macmillan.

ROYAL COMMISSIONERS (1884). *The Second Report of the Royal Commissioners on Technical Instruction*. London: HMSO.

SANDILANDS, A. (1971). 'A place to pool ideas', *The Teacher*, **17**, 23, 3.

SCHOOLS COUNCIL (1965). *Raising the School Leaving Age*. Working Paper No. 2.

SCHOOLS COUNCIL (1967). *Teachers' Groups and Centres*. Working Paper 10. London: HMSO.

SCHOOLS COUNCIL (1968). Enquiry 1. Young school leavers. London: HMSO.

SCHOOLS COUNCIL (1969). Foundation Stones (1966—68): an account by the Field Officers of the first two years' work of local curriculum development groups in a county authority. S. C. Pamphlet 3 (mimeographed).

SCHOOLS COUNCIL (1970). *Changes in School Science Teaching.* Curriculum Bulletin 3. London: HMSO.

SCHOOLS COUNCIL (1970). Teachers' Centres and the Changing Curriculum. A report on three National Conferences. Pamphlet No. 6 (mimeographed).

SCHOOLS COUNCIL (1972). Teachers' Centres and the Developing Curriculum: Aide Memoire to Schools Council Regional Study Conference held at Matlock College of Education (4—7 Jan 1972) (mimeographed).

SCHOOLS COUNCIL (1972). Teachers' Centres and the Developing Curriculum: Aide Memoire to Schools Council Regional Study Conference held at St. Osyths College of Education, Clacton (27—30 March 1972) (mimeographed).

SCHOOLS COUNCIL (1972). Teachers' Centres and the Developing Curriculum: Aide Memoire to Schools Council Regional Study Conference held at Rutherford College, University of Kent, Canterbury (18—21 July 1972) (mimeographed).

SCHOOLS COUNCIL (1973). *Pattern and Variation in Curriculum Development Projects*: A study of the Schools Council's approach to sixteen projects sponsored by the Council and other organizations. London: Macmillan Education.

SCHOOLS COUNCIL (1974). *Childrens Growth through Creative Experience* (Art and Craft Project, 8—13). Van Nostrand Reinhold: Wokingham.

SCHOOLS COUNCIL (1976). Project Profiles.

SILBERMAN, C. E. (1970). *Crisis in the Classroom.* New York: Random House.

SILVER, H. (1975). 'Since James. Interviews with Lord James, Roger Webster and James Porter', *Brit. J. of Teacher Educ.*, 1, 1, 3—17.

STEVENS, A. (1971). 'Centres for Action', *The Times Educ. Suppl.*, 2592.

STONE, R. J. (1975). 'Running a Maths Centre', *Mathematics Teaching,* **72,** 28—9.

THE TEACHER (1976). 'Centres saved', **29,** 20, 20.

THOMPSON, E. M. (1972). 'Teachers' centres: why they were established by the L.E.A.s instead of Institutes of Education', *Durham Research Review,* **6,** 29, 679.

THORNBURY, R. E. (Ed) (1973). *Teachers' Centres.* London: Darton, Longman and Todd.

TIMES EDUCATIONAL SUPPLEMENT (1976). 'Where the next axe may fall'. Article in 3210.

TOWN AND COUNTRY PLANNING ASSOCIATION. 'Closing the gap between the Schools Council and the Schools', *Bulletin of Environmental Education*, 39, 5—6.

TOWNSEND, H. E. R. and DEPARTMENT OF EDUCATION AND SCIENCE (1970). Statistics of Education Special Series No. 2. Survey of In-Service training for teachers 1967. London: HMSO.

UNIVERSITY OF LONDON, INSTITUTE OF EDUCATION (1971) Calendar of the University of London 1971—2.

UNIVERSITY OF LONDON INSTITUTE OF EDUCATION (1977) Spring/Summer Programme 1977 for the University Centre for Teachers.

WARDENS IN THE SOUTH EAST. (n.d.). The purpose and function of the Teachers' Centres in Teacher Education (mimeographed).

WARDENS IN THE SOUTH EAST (WISE) and LONDON UNIVERSITY (1971). Report of the First National Conference for Wardens of Teachers' Centres held at the Institute of Education, University of London, 19—21 April 1971. (mimeographed).

WARDENS IN THE SOUTH WEST and EXETER UNIVERSITY (1974). *CHANGE* (Eds. Dumpleton, J. and Stokes, C.) A symposium from the proceedings of the Fourth National Conference for Teachers' Centre Leaders (mimeographed).

WATKINS, R. (Ed) (1973). *In-Service Training: Structure and Content*. London: Ward Lock.

WORKSHOP CENTRE FOR OPEN EDUCATION (New York). (n.d) Information pamphlet.

WRIGHT, E. (1974). 'A strategic policy for Teachers' Centres', *Secondary Education*, 4, 2, 5—8.

BIBLIOGRAPHY

Suggestions for Related Reading

ANDREWS, L. O. (1976). 'Teaching techniques in the U.S.A. — The evolution of Professional Development Complexes', *Brit. J. of In-Service Educ.*, **2**, 2, 79—87.

ARNOLD, R. (1971). 'A centre in Britain', *Trends in Education*, **23**, 42—5.

BAKER, K. (1976). 'A review of current induction programmes for new teachers', *Brit. J. of In-Service Educ.*, **2**, 3, 179—86.

BALDWIN, W. A. (Ed) (1976). Teachers' Responsibility for Professional Development: Induction and Beyond. Bulmershe College of Higher Education Report on the ATO/DES Course arranged by the University of Reading School of Education, 1975—6. (mimeographed).

BATTEN, J. (1973). 'In-service education in teachers' centres: a suggested approach', *Journal of Curriculum Studies*, **3**, 1, 25—31.

BENNETT, G. (1975). 'Roles—teachers' centre warden', *Teachers' World*, 3444, 20.

BOLAM, R. (1975). 'Resources for INSET,' *Brit. J. of In-Service Educ.*, **2**, 1, 4—7.

BRADLEY, H. W. (1975). 'Regional committees. What must they do?', *Brit. J. of In-Service Educ.*, **2**, 1, 19—21.

BREARLEY, M., BROWSE, B., GODDARD, N. and KALLET, T. (1971/2) *Educating Teachers in British Primary Schools Today* London: Macmillan Education. (Also contained in Part 3 of *British Primary Schools Today*).

CASTON, G. (1974). 'The Schools Council in context', *The Journal of Curriculum Studies*, **3**, 1, 50.

CAVE, R. G. (1974). 'In-service education after the White Paper — an L.E.A. inspectors' viewpoint', *Cambridge J. of Educ.*, 4, 2, 52—9.

COUNCIL FOR EDUCATIONAL TECHNOLOGY FOR THE UNITED KINGDOM (nd) Education of Teachers and Trainers. Information Leaflet 2.

COUNCIL FOR EDUCATIONAL TECHNOLOGY FOR THE UNITED KINGDOM (nd) Resources for In-Service Education. Information Leaflet 4.

COUNCIL FOR EDUCATIONAL TECHNOLOGY FOR THE UNITED KINGDOM (nd) Educational Technology in Teacher Education and Training. Information Leaflet 8.

CRAWFORD, K. (1972). 'Wigan Teachers' Centre', *Education*, 139, 16,379.

CURRY, A. (1969). 'Teachers' centres', *Visual Education*, Aug/Sept., pp. 5—8 and 70—1.

DROPKIN, R. and TOBIER, A. (1972). Notes from Workshop Centre for Open Education. New York: (mimeographed).

DROPKIN, R. and TOBIER, A. (1974). The Workshop Centre Sampler. New York. (mimeographed)

DROPKIN, R. and WEBER, L. (1973). 'The City College Workshop Centre for Open Education', *Ideas*, 26, 13—8.

EDMONDS, E. L. (1967). 'Education for responsibility: fifty teacher staff colleges', *Brit. J. of Educ. Studies*, 15, 3, 243—52.

EDUCATION IN BUCKS (1969) 'Teachers' Centres', 21,2.

ELVIN, H. L. (1973). 'The White Paper: the choice before the colleges', *Education for Teaching*, 91, 2—6.

EVANS, E. (1970). 'Teachers, trainers and development centres', *Dialogue*, 6, 3.

FRENCH, A. (1974). 'Crawley Teachers' Centre,' *Dialogue*, 16, 12.

GIBSON, R. (Ed) (1972). The Professional Tutor. Cambridge Institute of Education. (mimeographed)

GOODACRE, E. J. (1974). L.E.A. Provision for Reading. Report of the 1970 Investigation into facilities provided by Local Education Authorities in England and Wales. New edition. Centre for the Teaching of Reading, School of Education, University of Reading.

GOUGH, R. G. (1973). 'Teachers' Centres. 1. Rachel McMillan Teachers' Centre', *Dialogue*, 15, p. 16.

GOUGH, R. G. (1975). 'Teachers' centres as providers of in-service education', *Brit. J. of In-Service Educ.*, 1, 3, 11—4.

HANSON, J. (1972). 'Curriculum Development is. . .', *Ideas*, 23, 6—10.

HARTLEY, A. (1973). 'Teaching for teachers', *The Guardian*, 29th May 1973.

HOLMES, B. (1972). 'Teacher education in Europe', *Secondary Education*, 2, 3, 3—6.

HOVE, O. (1968) *The System of Education in Norway*. Oslo: Ministry of Education and Johan Grundt Tanum Forlag.

HOWEY, K. R. (1976). 'Putting in-service teacher education into perspective', *Journal of Teacher Education*, 27, 2, 101—5.

HUBBARD, D. N. and SALT, J. (1972). 'Teachers' centres — some suggestions for a strategy', *Forum*, 14, 2, 63—4.

JONES, D. (1974). 'University of Surrey Teachers' Centre', *Dialogue*, 17, 16.

JORDAN, J. (1970). 'Change through a Teachers' Centre', Supplement to *Dialogue — School and Innovation 1870—1970*,' 14—5.

KAHN, H. (1972). 'Teachers' centres as agencies for change', *Ideas*, 23, 11—6.

KAHN, H. (1976). 'In-service education and teachers' centres', *Brit. J. of In-Service Educ.*, 2, 2, 100—2.

KERR, J. F. (Ed) (1969). *Changing the Curriculum*. London: University of London Press.

LEE, M. (1975). 'Teachers' centres and life-long education', *Brit. J. of In-Service Educ.*, 2, 1, 55—60.

LEEDS UNIVERSITY, INSTITUTE OF EDUCATION (1974). *Teacher Education: The Teachers' Point of View*. Slough: NFER.

MIDWINTER, E. C. (1970). *Nineteenth Century Education*. London: Longman.

MIDWINTER, E. C. (1974). 'Teachers' centres: the facilitators', *Brit. J. of In-Service Educ.*, 1, 1, 10—3.

MILES, M. (1974). 'The Schools Council and curriculum change in the modern world', *Secondary Education*, 4, 2, 54—6.

MILROY, C. P. (1975). 'The future of in-service education', *Brit. J. of In-Service Educ.*, 1, 2, 34—5.

MORANT, R. W. (1973). 'Professional centres need priority planning', *Education*, 142, 264—6.

MORANT, R. W. (1976). 'In-service priorities in a period of financial stringency', *Brit. J. of In-Service Educ.*, 2, 3, 144—9.

NATIONAL COUNCIL FOR INNOVATION IN EDUCATION (NORWAY). (nd) Structure and work of the Council. Ministry of Education: Oslo.

NATIONAL EDUCATION ASSOCIATION, INSTRUCTION AND PROFESSIONAL DEVELOPMENT (1973). Teacher Centred Professional Development. Washington D.C.: the Association (mimeographed).

NATIONAL EDUCATION ASSOCIATION (1973). In-Service Education

and Teacher Centres. Briefing Memo No. 3. Washington D.C.: the Association (mimeographed).

NATIONAL EDUCATION ASSOCIATION, INSTRUCTION AND PROFESSIONAL DEVELOPMENT (1974). Resources for In-Service Teacher Education. Washington D.C.: the Association.

NATIONAL UNION OF TEACHERS (1973). *The Induction of New Teachers.* London: NUT.

NIAS, J. (1974). 'Helping probationers — the role of the professional tutor', *Education 3—13*, **2**, 2, 116—121.

NYHAMAR, O. (1971). Education in Norway. Oslo, Royal Ministry of Foreign Affairs, Department of Cultural Relations.

O'BRIEN, T. (1975). 'Diary of a teachers' centre', *Mathematics Teaching*, **72**, 42—5.

PEPPER, R. (1972). 'In-service training and the Thomas Calton School, Peckham', *Forum*, **14**, 2, 50.

PERRONE, V. (1974). 'Open education: a perspective on where we've been, and where we are today', *Insights into Open Education*, **7**, 3. Centre for Teaching and Learning, University of North Dakota (mimeographed).

PRISELAC, N. J. and PRISELAC, S. M. (1976). 'Profile of a Functional Teacher Education Centre, 1975', *Brit. J. of In-Service Educ.* **2**, 2, 88—98.

READING AREA TRAINING ORGANISATION (1974). Professional Tutors in Schools. Reports from working parties in the Reading ATO. January — June 1974.

SCHOOLS COUNCIL. (1967) *Progress in Primary Mathematics.* Field Report 4. London: HMSO.

SCHOOLS COUNCIL. (1967) *Science in the Primary School.* Field Report 5. London: HMSO.

SCHOOLS COUNCIL (1969). First Year — An account of the work of a teachers' centre. London: The Council (mimeographed).

SCHOOLS COUNCIL (1969). *Mathematics in Primary Schools.* Curriculum Bulletin No. 1. Third Edition. London: HMSO.

SCHOOLS COUNCIL (1969). 'Workshop for ideas', *Dialogue*, **2**, 8—9.

SCHOOLS COUNCIL (1969). 'Round and about the teachers' centres', *Dialogue*, **2**, 10.

SCHOOLS COUNCIL (1969). 'Round and about the teachers' centres', *Dialogue*, **4**, 15.

SCHOOLS COUNCIL (1971). 'Teachers, trainers and development centres: miscellaneous reports', *Dialogue*, **7**, 10—1.

SCHOOLS COUNCIL (1971). 'Curriculum in the North West: initiatives and spin-offs', *Dialogue*, 7, 12—13.

SCHOOLS COUNCIL (1972). List of Teachers' Centres in England and Wales (mimeographed).

SCHOOLS COUNCIL (1974 and as amended Summer 1975) List of Teachers' Centres in England and Wales (mimeographed).

SCHOOLS COUNCIL (1974). *Dissemination and In-Service Training.* Pamphlet 14. Report of the Schools Council Working Paper on Dissemination, 1972—3.

SCHOOLS COUNCIL (1975). 'Teachers' Centres 4. Witton Park', *Dialogue*, 19, 14—5.

SCHOOLS COUNCIL (1975). 'Schools Council and local curriculum development', *Dialogue*, 20, 7.

THORNBURY, R. E. (1973). 'Powerhouses or postboxes', *Times Educ. Suppl.*, 3027.

THORNBURY, R. (1974). 'Teachers' centres', *New Society*, 28, 761—3.

UNIVERSITY OF READING SCHOOL OF EDUCATION (1972). Report of Comparative Education Tour to Gothenburg and Oslo. 2—15 April 1972.

WALTON, J. (1972). 'Teachers' centres: their role and function', *Forum*, 15, 1, 15—7.

WARDENS IN THE NORTH WEST AND KEELE UNIVERSITY INSTITUTE OF EDUCATION (1973). Report of the Third National Conference of Teachers' Centre Leaders/Wardens, Curriculum Development Officers and L.E.A. Advisory Staff, held at University of Keele, September 1973.

WARWICK, D. (1972). 'The Norse Code: Scandinavian in-service education', *Secondary Education*, 2, 3, 15—6.

WHITE, J. (1968). 'Instruction in obedience', *New Society*, 11, 292, 637—9.

WILLIAMS, L. (1971). 'The next step', *The Teacher in Wales*, 11, 5, 10—1.

YOUNG, M. F. D. (1972). 'On the politics of educational knowledge', *Economy and Society*, 11, 2, 194—215.

INDEX